Twisted Sisters Dumb Brothers

A Descriptive Analysis of the Fall of the Black Race
As We Once Knew It

by
James Reedom

Bloomington, IN   Milton Keynes, UK

authorHOUSE®

AuthorHouse™
1663 Liberty Drive, Suite 200
Bloomington, IN 47403
www.authorhouse.com
Phone: 1-800-839-8640

AuthorHouse™ UK Ltd.
500 Avebury Boulevard
Central Milton Keynes, MK9 2BE
www.authorhouse.co.uk
Phone: 08001974150

This book is a work of fiction. People, places, events, and situations are the product of the author's imagination. Any resemblance to actual persons, living or dead, or historical events, is purely coincidental.

First published by AuthorHouse 1/17/2007

ISBN: 978-1-4259-8665-0 (sc)

Printed in the United States of America
Bloomington, Indiana

This book is printed on acid-free paper.

TABLE OF CONTENTS

ACKNOWLEDGMENTS

The author wishes to thank all the positive brothers and sisters who have influenced his life. I wish to thank my mother and father, Dorothy and Marshall who guided me on a path of life to be a positive and open minded person in life. These two persons were children during the great depression and they were taught by their relatives how to survive. I wish to thank all of my twelve brothers and sisters especially: Margaret, Elizabeth, George, Marshall and Martha who providing me with positive role models to follow in life. Special gratefulness goes to my younger brothers and sisters, Gloria, John, Dorothy, Frances, Robert and Jackie who provided me with a conscience to really understand what life is really all about. Special Thanks goes to my Uncles Put, Wilfred, and Patrick and Daniel my brother in law for providing me with wonderful stories about life and assisting me with developing a positive attitude of life. Finally, a special thanks go to My Aunt Lillian from New Orleans who was always there for my family and to the Pat sisters, Cleo, Alex and the black University/College system Grambling, Southern and Fisk as trusted educational family friends and confidents.

GLOSSARY

Twisted Brothers – Bozo brothers who have no attitude of what being a real man is all about.

Twisted Sisters – Twisted sisters can be defined as black females who have lived a topsy turvy life in which they do not know how to tell good people from bad ones.

Plastic Brothers and Sisters – Individuals who are phony and they have no perception of what it means to be a real person when dealing with life's problems

Baby Zoë – The final product of a mom and dad who have no vision of how to raise and train a child.

Momma Zoë – She had no prescriptive vision of what it means to be a good mother and a real African Queen

Daddy Zoë – He has no prescriptive vision of what it means to be a father and how to be held accountable and responsible for his actions as a father.

Skizer – Blacks who like to use and manipulate each other and innocent people

Dumb Brother – A brother who has no class and style and sense of character of what a real man is all about

Dumb Sister – A sister who has no class and style and wants to stay at the same level of development in life; whereby she lets the world pass her by.

White Shadow Brothers and Sisters – Brothers and sisters who want to be white

Black Widow Spider – A sister who drives her husband and man to death by working him hard just to get money from his insurance and other assets. She never really loved him.

Duby – East Coast former term for a dollar

Benjamin – Street slang term for a $100 bill

Baby Making Stud – A brother who enjoys making babies just for bragging rights-He has no notion of taking care of the child.

Yellow – Light Complexion Sisters-Sisters who look white and can pass for white-they are very confused.

Yellow Light Complexion Brothers – Brothers who look white and can pass for white and they are very confused.

Mandingo Brothers – Dark Skinned Athletic Brothers with a serious attitude

Mrs. Robinson – Wives who plays around

Mr. Robinson – Husbands who plays round

Bopper – a woman who moves from man to man for money

And Sraggin – A new term for the new young blacks-with dropping baggy clothes and a negative attitude.

Paw Paws – Older men who love being used by young women and boppers. They give them lots money and assistance.

Chapter 1

INTRODUCTION

The black race as we know it; is now at a standstill. The key notion here is that twisted brothers and sisters have brought the race to a paradoxical level. Our race as it exists today is no longer the proud race as we once knew it. The race of strong men like King, Marshall, Malcolm X, Mohammad Ali, Booker T. Washington, W.E. Dubois, Marshal Reedom, My late father, and others have now become a race of thugs and weasels who think that they are men. They have no class and culture and are hostile and angry men who are not even one tenth of what we used to be. We are angry with the system and we do not even know why. We mistreat our women and take our angry hostilities out on them. The black male as he is known, today is an endangered species. He is totally lost and he has no way to turn but to take it out on his woman. I have known so many brothers who are very hostile and are unwilling to be open and honest in the way that they relate and interact with people. This is very depressing given the fact that they do not treat their sisters and other black males with self respect. I have noticed that so many black man and black females are angry and quick to argue with individuals for no apparent reason other than the fact that they are upset with someone and or something. This is apparent in the way that they walk around with a hostile attitude. The black race, as I see it is undergoing a tremendous transition in the way that we treat and deal with each other. But one thing is unequivocal and very clear: there is a problem with the way that black males and females treat each other and it is interacting with the kids and our families and unless something is done to correct this problem blacks will be having difficult times a head in the way that we treat each other; and the race as a whole will be doomed for failure. This particular analysis attempts to look at those salient issues and variables which contribute to focus on these negative attitudes and attempts to identify through cases studies where these attitudes came from; and tries to examine what effective strategies can be utilized to correct them; and in essence offer some prescriptive solutions for positive development. Over time, we have collected through case studies some observations which maybe critical in our understanding why these attitudes exist and what can be done to change them.

It is hard for some people to understand that the anger which some young brothers and sisters have had within themselves for a long time; to understand the problems which blacks are confronted with because of their lack of understanding of the system. The most problematic situation that blacks face is that someone; namely systematic simulation experts have placed in their minds negative thoughts, feelings and desires that they are their own worst enemies and that they should dislike and try to destroy each other. This is a sad commentary considering the notion that both black males and females are quick to pull the trigger on each other for blaming each other with being the root causes of their problems. Neither one wants to be held accountable and responsible for their actions and the way that they ought to react to problematic situations. Sisters sometimes put their heads into the sand like the ostrich and refused to deal with their problems and or the negative surroundings around them. Brothers on the other hand are angry individuals who are selfish and they exhibit a behavior in which they only think about themselves. This abnormal behavior on the part of the negative brother creates a serious problem of communication between he and his female counterpart which forces her to adapt some of his negative behavior; in essence what we have occurring within the black race is what I am transcribing now as a failure to communicate. This failure of communication has created a negative void in the way that positive black males and females ought to correspond with each in a harmonious relationship pattern with females which contributes to the positive stability and awareness of the personal growth and stability of the male-female relationship. Unfortunately, the way that these inherent relations among the black female and her man as they exist, today, it appears that nothing positive is every going to happened. How did this negative annihilation of the black race as we once knew it come about? Who is responsible for the destruction of the once proud black race which is rich in cultural heritage and riches of social awareness and several worthy contributions to society? When did it start and how was it resurrected? Let us now start the journey of how this become a reality and analyze what can be done to correct it before the black race is doomed forever and eventually is on its way for total destruction and becoming a footnote in the history of western civilization.

When Did It Start?

The annihilation started in 1968. This was the time that blacks through the civil rights movement under the leadership of Martin Luther King Jr. started to seek the acquisition of their civil rights and liberties as full fledged American citizens. It was the best of times and it was also the worst of times. In the quest for the acquisition of equality and rights black males faced so many obstacles. First, of all, it started with the advent of the Women Lib Movement of 1972, the system solved the problem of racial equality by getting a black female and a woman into the jobs and economic development structure of the system; in the meantime the black man was pushed back from total acquisition of his rights. What did some sisters do?

1. They looked down on a brother because he did not make as much money as she did.

2. She became a part of the problem instead of the solution because instead of her working with her brother to make him better she started to form coalitions with her white female counterparts some of which whom were avid lesbians and they created a game plan to destroy all men; it did not matter what race or color he was. This perpetuation of radical feminism led to some sisters misunderstanding of what their real role in society is. It is important to note that once a sister begins to advance the concept that no man is necessary and sufficient to her survival that we are entering a "dark hole" in the relationships between black males and females in society.

3. The implementation of the "I am smarter than a man attitude and all brothers are dumb theory. This notion on the part of sisters have destroyed many a black man's character and his self esteem level more than any of the other negative things that society has perpetuated. Once a man's ego and self esteem is destroyed by his own woman; he feels that he is of no value to himself and his family. In reality, brothers started to feel that sisters had betrayed them and the civil rights movement all together.

4. The failure of brothers and sisters to communicate led brothers to seek comfort and ego building and total self awareness and fulfillment with the company of others races especially white females; because she was in a power and money struggle of power positioning within our society with her white male counterpart. For the most part these coalitions were good ones because they had a tendency to provide

society with a new cultural awareness that all people can contribute to the worthy ness of society. But some where along the way some of the sisters and brothers got too greedy and in a very systematic and well devised and calculated scheme only begin to look after themselves and they forget from where they came from.

5. The implementation of the" Crab and Crawfish Theory" this is the theory that perpetuates that as soon as one crab and or crawfish tries to get out of the bucket that you have one or several other crabs who try to hold them back in to the bucket. This theory has been used to define and explain the reason why blacks cannot work with each other and that they cannot in essence relate to each other and get along together.

6. Most blacks are reluctant to want to assist and or help and work with each other. It seems that they have an inherent dislike for the way that some blacks are trying to be successful in dealing with life.

7. The perpetuation of the "ROSCOE Theory". What is the ROSCOE Theory? The ROSCOE Theory states that ROSCOE is a black person who has little and or no self esteem in what they can do in life. These ROSCOE proponents are black people who believe that they are equal to other black persons with the implementation of that notion; that they are equal in all aspects of life to others but yet they are unwilling to make the initial sacrifices which are necessary to become successful. The main problem with ROSCOE is that they seem to be unhappy in the way that they deal with life. I know of a ROSCOE person once who destroyed a billion dollar business operation because they possessed pure jealously and hate; they believed that what is yours is mine. In our race, we have to be careful and on guard with ROSCOE people they have no heart and no conscience when it comes to destroying positive functions within our society and the black sub community. Our community is at a serious standstill because people who can make an impact in the way that black society is deteriorating; at an unlimited level of systematic sub community self destruction level are refusing to take charge and start making worthy contributions to our black society as a whole. One only has to look at their next door neighbor and within their own family structures to identify things that are not normal with our race. We, namely black people are afraid of our own people

and we do not even trust each other. I am amazed how unhappy some of our black people are and how they want to make a quick dollar and try to mimic and steal ideas from each other. This is a sad commentary considering how we once were a proud and dedicated people such is not the case today.

Chapter 2

TWISTED SISTERS DEFINED

Twisted sisters can be defined as black females who have lived a topsy turvy life in which they do not know good people from bad ones. A lot of their problems stems from the fact that they have lived a lot of their life listening to the wrong persons and they therefore are put into a position whereby they constantly make mistakes. In my, life time I have met a lot of twisted sisters. Some examples, of twisted sisters are:

Mimi

Mimi – A black female who was the graduate of a black college in Mississippi. She was constantly pulling guns on men that was just as twisted as she was. Here was a college trained individual who could not control her emotions and she was just as hostile as any twisted sister could be in her daily personal dealing with men. Mimi met a guy by the name of Roscoe who by himself will be given special attention in this book in a later discussion; but for all practical purposes we want to continue to discuss Mimi. Mimi had two beautiful homes and a nice job but her relationships with men were twisted and unimaginable. She invited Roscoe to come and live with her after she was rejected by me. The twisted nature of their relationship was not of a sexual nature; it was more of one whereby he was her house boy. As part of his keep Roscoe was to keep the house cleaned and wash dishes. In Mimi's eyes Roscoe was nothing more than a house boy. Roscoe had low self esteem. This was odd considering how he himself had a high degree of training and a corporate background. She eventual replaced him with a yellow preacher who was more suitable for her dominant nature and personality. It is important to note that Mimi was a typical sister who had a huge temper within herself. I believe that earlier in life that she had been hurt and that she carried this drama within her self for a very long time. A most important point which can be advanced here is that some sisters believe in revenge and this type of negative attitude leads them not to trust anyone and or anybody.

Other Reflections On Mimi and Roscoe's Relationship

1) Both individuals did not trust anyone.

2) Roscoe was hurt because his marriage had gone bad.

3) Mimi because she had experienced personal hurt in life could return love and affection to any man.

4) Both lovers had a false vision and a serious misinterpretation of what life was really all about. Simply stated neither one of them wanted to face the truth and dance to the right music. They had a serious void in understanding of what life was really all about and this notion had a tendency to provide them with a negative understanding of life and relationships.

This attitude is typical of most brothers and sisters who engage in relationships in which they are not comfortable with the way that they both bring excess baggage to their social relationship. The driving force around a positive relationship is the man and the woman adding trust and complete understanding and openness to the deal. Mimi and Roscoe's relationship created a situation in which neither party was willing to establish a positive bond and organized structuralized goals for a positive commitment in their relationship. In essence, now the notion can be advanced that their relationship was doomed to failure from the start; due to the parties, Mimi and Roscoe unwillingness to be open and honest to each other.

Asil

Asil – was an attractive fair skinned sister; she was from a large southern town, I first met Asil when I became her business consultant and I was assisting her with setting up her beauty salon business. Asil was bright and articulate but her main problem was that she was a plotter. She was not real and everything about her was a game. She married a brother who was an insurance man and she liked him because he had a gaming personality too. It is amazing how so many of our sisters are attracted to men who are on their way to Jail University. Asil had a high degree of potential but she just could not get rid of her attraction to Jail University men. Asil was also bi-sexual and she was in love with another sister beautician Hifil who eventually ended up on drugs. Both of these sisters were highly attractive; it made me sick to my stomach to observe such beautiful African Queens relegating themselves to being sub standard and average sisters. I often wondered why this was happening; and questioned what were the root causes of this reality ; and posing the question whether this was a mere illusion of a detrimental element of our twisted spawning with in our community male and female relationships. Asil has now divorced with no kids and she is still playing her game.

Mazel

Mazel was Asil sister, she was a fashion designer by trade but her main problem was that she lived a sheltered life and that in itself was a problem with her adjustments in life due through her making the wrong decisions. She was a kind person; due to the fact that she had so many twisted people in her family; it made it hard for reality to be part of her life. Mazel eventually left town for a little while because she was ashamed that her father had been caught fencing stolen items; after some Hispanic guys had robbed an armored truck. The family name and reputation had been severely damaged. But later on she moved back and opened up a sophisticated candy store in smooth town. She appears to be doing well now. I must admit that Mazel tried in several ways to fight her twisted ness but in the end she gave in because of the strong family and peer pressures that she had to bear. What factors led to Mazel and Hifil developing a bi-sexual relationship? There are several factors which led to the women developing a bi-sexual down low relationship:

1) Mazel loved men so much that she became tired with dealing with all of them together.

2) Mazel was a drama queen and a constant user and manipulator of men and women.

3) Her working in the beauty salon and cosmetic industry kept her in daily contact with women from all walks of life.

4) She had a high intensity sexual appetite for both men and women; which made her a 5th degree serious bi-sexual female.

5) She was highly attracted to hi-fil because she was from the poor sides of the tracks. Hifil exemplified the bad and Mazel the good.

Dee

Dee was a sister from a metropolitan city on the east coast. Although, Dee was an attractive female who possessed a manipulative personality which enabled her to control men. Sometimes, she could be as gentle as she wanted to be when she associated with positive people; but when she was around weak people; Dee became a different animal. Dee was a highly educated and sophisticated but very unhappy and twisted female. I, first met Dee at a party with several persons; in which I was invited to cook Louisiana Gumbo and seafood dishes for her entourage. Later Dee and her roommate Lady G and I became friends because we all seemed to be attracted to positive working friendships. I was shocked and startled when she, Dee asked me to become her pimp. She told me Man, I know that you will see to it that I get of my money. I stated to her Dee you are too good of a person to sell yourself like that. I cannot do this; that was my initial reaction and response to her out of bounds request. I never saw or heard from Dee every again. She just got lost in the cracks. Dee was a graduate of one of the top ten technological schools in the country.

The Church Lady

The Church Lady – was a beautician and a self proclaimed holistic healer. She was a member a holiness church which was located somewhere in Smooth, Texas. Her father was an alcoholic who constantly beat up on her. She was an ex gang member who left the gang after she saw so many of her friends dying and or who ended up in the hospital; she had severe and voluminous problems of twist ness. She eventually had a baby for a basketball player from a black university whom she thought was going to the NBA (National Basketball Association; Mr. Wonderful was from a southern state; he did not want her and she become hostile towards men in every sense. In essence; every man was the devil and she made each man know it too. She once tried to run her boyfriend down with a car cause, he told her that she needed to get her life together and become more positive. Dee is still in the church and is raising her son to think just like her in their complicated dealing with life.

Lashinda

Lucinda was a sorority sister and she had an arrogant attitude. She was definitely a "gold digger "who only wanted a man who had some money; but she because of her arrogance she kept hooking up with no good brothers. She had a propensity for wearing nothing but red clothes items. Shinda had a huge attitudinal problem in that she looks down on certain brothers; in essence when she herself and her mother could not keep a man. She seems to have huge relationship problems in the way that she dealt with a man. In essence, she was another sister with a serious attitude. She was also, jealous of other good looking sisters because she wanted to be the center of all attention. Simply speaking she was a drama queen and a royal pain in the butt. She was what most brothers would call a sister with a bull's eye" and she must be avoided at all costs.   Life was not kind to Shinda because she chased a lot of positive people away from her life.   In the end it was her negative and hostile attitude which destroyed the very essence of Shinda living a positive and productive life.

Jeanette – The Black Widow Spider

She was a lady who had buried two husbands. Jeanette was a very unhappy educated female who put a lot of aggressive and program strain on a man. She typifies sisters who husband and or man dies as a result of the sister are not willing to let up on her demands and requests to him. In another observation, I noticed Jeanette tried to interfere in her son's life too. He was having his share of dysfunctional problems because his Mexican girlfriend was pregnant for him. Both the mother and the son enjoyed entertaining their friends at home during family hours. Jeanette's greatest joy was shopping for furniture and future husbands on Saturdays.

Victoria

Victoria is the imaginary white female who loves brothers no more than for the reasons to destroy them and keep him from his woman. Her main goal and objective is to keep separate him from his woman and to make him weak in order that he is of no value and usage to any one. Many brothers have relationships with white females and these white females have a certain aggressive attitudes which breed superiority into them; On the other hand they feel that sisters are inadequate. These brothers feel that the white female is superior for the following reasons:

1. She is smarter than the black female.

2. She lets him have his way with her.

3. Just being seen with her creates a wonderful feeling of superiority and great karma-which conveys total fulfillment.

4. She has more money than a sister and she understands the white majority system much better.

5. She allows a bother to be put into hog's heaven by letting have his way

Other Points Concerning Victoria:

Victoria came from a large Midwestern town in which there were not a lot of black people. I believe her fascination with the black male came from her desiring the forbidden fruit, namely brothers. One good thing that I noticed about white females is that they are just as attracted to dumb brothers as there are to smart ones. They are also attracted to athletic brothers to the extend that he is going to get a professional sports contract and or he is a college star. But the contention remains that if he the black man cannot become her meal ticket than she has no need or use for him. But I have found that some sisters who are all for a brother; if he lies good and makes promises to her that that he cannot keep. Victoria believes that once you go" white"; she knows that the brother will never go back to his sister again. For all, practical purposes she is right.

Lucy

She was from a small town in the South and she was divorced. By trade, Lucy was a professional legal secretary. She had a serious problem with men after her divorce from her husband who went for a newer model. Lucy was an excellent business person but she kept looking for love in all the wrong places. She was a stylish intelligent good looking lady but she was always dealing with loser lawyers and deadbeat brothers. She went from being a good housewife with a bad husband to dealing with loser lawyers. Lucy was a church lady who directed choirs and wrote music for many churches. She eventually married a man who was on his way out and she moved to a large Texas town. What was really wrong with Lucy that made her twisted? One of the main problems that Lucy experienced was that she had been re-programmed by her husband Floyd X to become a different person from the kind person that she once was. For example, she became bitter towards all men. Lucy had a propensity not to trust any man. She started to adopt an attitude that all men was her enemy and that they had to be taught a lesson. The main problem with her attitude is that she became a player in a game of love and relationship in which she was not qualified to play. In the final analysis the person who was destroyed was Lucy, herself. Lucy also, has a daughter named Meka. Both mother and daughter never got along and they were constantly in competition for men. Meka would always tell her mother's suitors all of her mothers intimate secrets just to upset her mother. Just for the record; Meka was a college cheer leader by trade.

Escobedo

Escobedo was the southern high yellow complexion daughter of a television owner of a southern state. She had a lot of mental and emotional problems and she went "Deep South" in to a mental nervous break down after her father and her ex husband had been caught dealing with drugs through their television station in the south. Escobedo's problems originated when she married Jason, who was a curly hairy yellow playboy. Escobedo loved him immensely until she found out that he was sampling the carnal delights of all her girlfriends. First, she Escobedos tried to reform her philandering husband, Jason, because she still loved him; but she finally gave up on him once she found that she could not change him. Her main technique in trying to get a man that she liked was to lock him up in a room and read him from two versions of the bible: The Roman Catholic version and the King James versions. Her twisted ness led to her having a mental breakdown later. One point about Escobedos that must be pointed out is that she loved "older men" who were her sugar daddies on the side. She had a constant flow of them and they were all rich men. One in particular was one of the richest black men in both the East and West Coasts.

Renee (1)

Renee was a very emotional lady with a lot of drama problems. She had lived in both California and the south. She eventually becomes the owner of her own ministry. Renee passed herself off as a freaky lady who would do any and everything to get what she wanted and what she needed. Her husband Melvin developed cancer and she said that she was going to nurse him; I suspect that she wanted to get his insurance money. Renee was typical of a lot of twisted sisters in that she has lost sight of what the differences between a good man and a bad man are. She took delight in dating both men and women. She had a special fondness for any young man to corrupt them on one hand but when she became bored with them she wanted the older guys to swoon over her and pay all her bills and living expenses. She was one of the sisters who would always state: that I can tell when a brother is weak; these are the brothers that she would pounce on and abuse. Simply stated, her theory was that a weak man will give a twisted sister every thing that she wants and that she could use and abuse him to the max. One thing about Renee which was unique; she loved dating paw-paws. This is a unique theory considering the fact that "paws-paws" will pay the bills; but sisters must understand that paw paw can be more jealous and more deadlier in his unbridled passions than a young man. Ladies beware deal with him at your own risk.

Renee (2)

She was fat and dumpy and out of shape she lived her whole live around a thug named Mopad. The more that he dogged her and abused her; the greater that she loved it. Mopad was also having a relationship with her cousin, Tee Ca. His greatest asset was that he stayed in and out of jail a lot. He was known for the way that he carried himself but many considered him to have a brain the size of a Pea. But Renee seemed to be a glutton for punishment. She wanted to be dogged for no apparent reason other than she liked it. This twisted sister's problem could have stemmed from the fact the she has a high degree of low self esteem due to her dealing with the wrong fellows. It also seemed that more full figured that she got; the more her self esteemed level dropped which caused her to date more losers and abuser dumb brothers.

Salome

Salome was the daughter of a minister and the wife of a minister. She had a master's degree in real estate and she worked for a bank. Later on she took a government corporation position. She had a problem with keeping a good man and she loved money and would do any and everything for it. Salome was a high yellow sister who loved money and manipulation more than being an honest and a fair person. She even taught her daughters the game of money manipulation. Her game was to pursue men to gain as much as she could out of them. This lady also dated white guys too. She enjoyed using them to her own advantage. She had used her knowledge of the black ministry to manipulate men for various reasons. She was a twisted sister of the highest magnitude.

Aanom

She was a good con artist and she had lived in California and she was another sister who had a problem keeping a good man. Everything about Aanom was about running and operating a con game against brothers. The key to her life style was that she came from a dysfunctional family with its share of tragedies and malfunctions:

1. Her sister had died in a fire

2. Her husband was a player

3. She was on the street playing the game since she was 16 years old

4. She had an affinity for falling for loser type men. The real problem with Aanom was that she had been beaten so many times by her first husband that she lost sight of what life was really all about. In essence, her loved for the street live and her weaknesses of the flesh and fame made her a prime candidate for systematic failure. She was a strange person given the fact that one moment she could be nice and loving and in a matter of a few seconds she would become a rattlesnake person with a deadly venom to destroy all life. Aanom also had a daughter named Mandra and a granddaughter named Chastity. It seemed that the vicious circle of bad relationships continued with the family because both Mandra and Chastity continued to manifest the same dysfunctional traits of the Mother and Grandmother more problems of twisted ness and the innate ability to deal with life in a positive manner.

Patricia

She loved men that had been to the joint. She came from a long line of females who had been abused in their lives and they did not see much open for the future. This is an unpleasant state of affairs because she had no hope for a bright future. Patricia's outlook for the future was bleak because her mother was a con artist whose con games caught up with her; and one day she had been paid back for all the wrong doings which she had done to others. Patricia in essence was a victim and she fell through the cracks to become the same person as her mother a twisted sister with a life of being enslaved in a bottle with no where to go and no place to turn to. There is no greater love that a mother can give to a daughter and or her other offspring than to teach them how to love others, themselves and to make positive contributions to society. In this case, Patricia could not give her offspring what they needed the most her greatest give of parental love and the ability to be a positive role model.

Young Lady

She was the daughter of Patricia and she was taught by both her mother and her grandmother on how to use her looks and her body to get what she wanted. Later on she ended up with a babyfrom a dead beat brother. She had been trained by both Anom and her mother, Patricia to be a young user and hustler whose sole objective was to get even with men.

Tiffany

One of the best con artists in the business. She taught her daughter to become a hustler. Later on she became a troubled young lady with an outstanding looks and a beautiful body. When it was all over Tiffany's daughter ended up doing a stretch of time in a southern jail. Her daughter blamed everybody for her problems except herself. This was a direct result of Tiffany who sold her self for anything and everything; in essence, Tiffany daughter believed that she was some of the rudimentary causes of her problems. Parents have to realize that children emulate their every move such is common with the offspring of twisted children; the kids have a tendency to copy their parents on all levels of development. Although they have the ability to develop their own character and personality traits some of them in the end just like apples that fall from the tree; Our children became just like their parents systematic losers.

Tiffany's Daughter – Apples Donot Fall To Far From The Tree

Tiffany's daughter was provided with every opportunity to become successful. But like all members of the "hip hop and rap generation"; she had a total disregard and respect for the system of power and order in society; when it was all over she ended up doing a stretch in a southern penal institution. She blamed everybody for her problems except herself. She learned the game from her mother Tiffany and later on became the ultimate twisted con artist which made her a first class student for Jail University. Does she have a future? I believe that she does not because once a twisted sister has tasted the life of being in jail university to develop a tendency to want to become of a criminal mind than before their entrance in to the jail fraternity/sorority. The strange phenomena which exist here demands that we understand that the mind is a terrible thing to waste. This used to be the motto of the Negro College Fund. The ultimate reality here is that once a person becomes a graduate of Jail University; they no longer have a thirst for living a positive. It now time for them to start their new life; a recurrence of a new and negative orientation to a life of crime.

Jewels' – She Loved Her Ladies

She was a radio news person from the South. Later on she became a troubled young lady due to her negative indiscretions. She had the looks and the body; but when it was all over she ended up doing a stretch of time in a southern jail. She blamed every body for her problems while she refused accept full accountability for her actions. She was a bi sexual lady who had a fondness for other females. She was called jewels for hard dark beautiful skinned.

Cleo

Cleo was a high yellow female who loved money and fame and status more than anything else. She loved to use brothers because of her creole upbringing. She married an attorney who was a tall gangly type of fellow who she never really loved; but she married him for what she really wanted most out of life money and security. One has to understand the nature of creole sisters; they are twisted on their beauty and they feel that all men want to seek and desire them. This can lead to their ultimate downfall for sisters like Cleo because in the end it was her beauty vainness which ultimately destroyed her.

LaMede

LeMede was a Jehovah Witness who had a real problem with understanding men. She was like an ice princess and part of it had to do with her upbringing; both of her parents were educators. Lemede was the first twisted sister that I had ever met in my life. I notice how confused that she was and how it was hard for her to cope with life and things of social awareness. She was a brilliant student in math but had no common sense; I believe that part of it was that she was from a small town and maybe she Lemede had religious training difficulties to deal with. But I would never forget the face; a face and look which I have seen on many twisted sisters throughout my travels. The face of confusion and disillusionment.

My Beau

Beau was a high yellow Creole lady. She was another high yellow with a twisted mind. She had a college degree in English in which she used to travel down the amazon later on she went back home to stay on the farm with her mother Mercedes. Beau became what in some circles is labeled as a perennial old maid and busy body with a college degree.

Blue Bell

Blue Bell's Mother was on drugs and later on she got hooked too. Blue Bell was from the southern Midwest. She came from a twisted family in which there were no strong male figures in the house. Every man had either been in jail and or on Americas Most wanted (smile).

Angie

Angie was a cheer leader and she was Lucy's Daughter. A child of divorce she blamed her mother for the break up of their family. She constantly did things to rebel against her mother. She smoked dope among other things later on she herself got pregnant. These turn of events in Angela's life seem strange considering the fact that she and her mother were identical twins in the way that they copied each others moves. Ultimately, the lives and tragedies of mother and daughter become one in that they shared ultimate failure together.

Lady P

Lady P was a well educated sister from the Midwest. She was a divorcee whose husband was a player. The main problem with their situation was that they relationship had a negative effect on the children. The mother smoked weed, the ex husband smoked and all of the yellow daughters smoked. This was a unique twisted ness given the fact that all the members of the family were highly educated. Lady P was a corporate administrator who made in excess of $175,000-$250,000 a year. She was freakier than her daughters and she had an abundance of high energy and motivation but she still kept falling in love with twisted brothers.

Theresa

Theresa was a talented high school student who worked for the county government in a southern state. Later on she because associated with a drug dealer named Dead man who eventually became her pimp. She had three kids. Because of her drug habits she eventually became a courier for drug dealers; one day she spent some their dope money. They called her on the phone and told her to come out; or they were going to take care of her whole family. When she came out they took her to a rock house and made her smoke rock all night long. She caught a heart attack in the house. The dealers than took her to the south side of town and threw her in a ditch. Theresa was 26 years old. She had lived a life of prostitution and drugs. Could she have been saved? I doubt it; Theresa was doomed to failure from the start because she had a weakness for bozo brothers. In our race we have so many of our young girls and women who are controlled by their peer groups, the media, mother and men. All of these factors lead to a lonely and difficult life. One only has to look upon the faces of these sisters to observe the following:

1. Confusion

2. Unhappiness

3. Disillusion

4. Anger

5. Rage

6. Open hostility towards men

There are many variables within the mental psyche of the twisted sister which might contribute to this phenomenon happening but I believe that in Theresa's case it was her male demons who took over and controlled her life and eventually she became a casualty of life. It appears that falling through the cracks finally did her in.

Chapter 3

MRS. ROBINSON

The married sister who loves cheating on her husband can be defined as Mrs. Robinson. There are many reasons why sisters cheat. Some of the reasons that they give are:

1. My husband does not pay attention to me anymore.

2. My husband is not making enough money.

3. My Man does not measure up.

4. My Man is a cheater

5. My man does not talk to me and stimulate my mind.

But the real reason that Mr. Robinson cheats is that she wants too. She believes that she should get what she wants and what she really needs. This is an interesting revelation given the fact that she derives some type of twisted power from manipulating both her man and the other woman's' man in a well organized and deliberate scheme to gain power in a relationship and to keep it. It is amazing on how these sisters have developed an attitude in which they are trying to be like their male counterparts who are cheating husbands. There is no joy in using deceit and deception in a relationship because it creates several bad feelings in the family structure:

1. Children, if they exist are hurt in the way that the family is malfunctioning because of Mrs. Robinson indiscretions

2. The male and the female have a tendency to engage in combative and acrimonious relations. This can have a negative effect on their children and or offspring and greatly inhibit there developmental growth.

3. The female may carry aggressive and hostile relations feelings in the way that she deals with her husband and male counterpart which may lead to an unnatural female freakish behavior.

4. Freakish behavior in a wife may led to her becoming very unstable and her offspring may adopt some of her unnatural lifestyles which may lead to her having serious emotional problems later on which can become a contributing factor to her being seriously unstable in all of her relationships later on. One central point in Mrs. Robinson development is that she has the potential to keep her family together and to save her children; but she must relinquish her desire for negative fulfillment at the sacrifice of losing control over her loved ones and the ability to save the black family in her role as a true queen instead of trying to be queen freak and compete with other women who have no value and substance in life. Mrs. Robinson must realize that her untimely actions as the negative female in this twisted family structure is contributing to the destruction of the very underlying fiber of the family systematic unit which has stabilized black people together for years. Mrs. Robinson has to come to grips with the realization that she is a central point to stabilization of the black family within the sub community. If she continues to have problems with the socialization process she will make it more difficult for her race to survive. The real problem with Mrs. Robinson lies in the fact that she is totally happy with the way that her life is going. She is oblivious to her surroundings that she does not care how things are going on in her life. One of the key elements of Mrs. Robinson life style is that she is totally satisfied. This is due to a large part of Mrs. Robinson belonging to a new breed of twisted sisters who want to make their man pay for all the previous wrongs committed against her by other men. She tries to manipulate men in her life to gain a partisan advantage over them. But there is one point that Mrs. Robinson must realize if she wants to co-exist within the sub community: What goes around comes around comes around. It is very important that Mrs. Robinson and other women of her class and life style realize that no one and especially black females should feel that they have to stoop to the level of negativity in relationships with their male counterparts and that sisters like Mrs. Robinson are daily experimenting with. It is high time that these women go back to the drawing board and become the decent females that they once were and take back their families and save the children.

Chapter 4

MS. UNIVERSITY

The University woman can be defined as a dominant sister who controls her man by having more education than him. This is the woman who feels that the Blackman does not have enough education for her. University females have a unique ability to make worthy contributions to society; It is an acknowledged fact throughout history that we have used the university lady to set up a strong moral fiber and assist us with the cognitive understanding, creative physical, and mental development of our family structure to create and implement a strong mental- social fiber bond with our children. Everyone has had a teacher like Ms. M who was a role model for both the young black student in the way that she properly developed them as a person. I can vividly remember how the teachers and educators of old had tried to mold you in to becoming a person of substance who could contribute to society as a worthy person who had something of substance. Such is not the case to day, because what we now have in our community: is nothing more than a bunch of greedy and grubby females who are trying to use education as a tool to get:

1. Get what they want-at any time regardless of what it involves and no matter who it hurts

2. They seem to strive to seek what they and when they want it-at all costs-no matter what they have to do to achieve and or acquire it.

3. They have a sense of urgency that by utilizing the notion: by any means necessary-to justify unreasonable wants and desires

The most depressing thing about the new University sisters is that they do not have the brains or the intellect of the old university sisters because in essence their game is one of manipulating and trying to get over. I have known many wonderful, creative and talented university females in my life but I have come to the conclusion that all of these sisters seem to be attracted to bad men. There is something strange about black female educated and corporate women who are attracted to undesirable men. I have tried over the years to figure out what is this attraction of black females to bozo men. I hope that may be some of these observations may shed some light on this discussion:

1. Some sisters seem to love lying brothers. The more you lie the more she wants to reform you; are be with you.

2. They are attracted to dishonest brothers

3. The dishonest brother is seriously desired by them

4. Brothers without a future are a luxury item because sisters can manipulate him and discard him at anytime within the relationship.

5. The user brother attracts them

6. The Gigolo Brother is a must

7. Brothers with no morale fiber and values in life are attractive to the twisted educational and corporate sister.

Chapter 5

FREAK WOMAN

The worst kind of woman that a man could know is a tramp, trollop, manipulator or prostitute. She was taught since a child by her mother, sisters and aunties who were her big sister- Her mother who had her at 15 years of age; the ladies in order to survive both learn how to roll and use men together. Freak woman was born from a dysfunctional family- a family in which none of the men stayed. It was clear that some of the women in the family had sexually been molested at some point and or another. The men or male figures in the family were constantly going in and out of jail like a revolving door and they had no substance or reason for living in life and or enjoying the positive aspects of life. Freak woman's Mother had been in and out of drug rehab houses and she was a professed alcoholic. She had relationships with men whereby she would wake up in the mornings the day after and wonder who she was with and how he got there.

Observations About Freak Lady

1. She had bi sexual tendencies

2. She knew how to roll and control men

3. She had a wonderful pleasing personality-which she integrated as part of her male con game.

4. She had a tendency to want to assist people with problems while she herself had low self esteem problems and was incapable of assisting others.

5. She had emotional problems which seem to overwhelm her at times but she continued to try to solve them on her own. Freak Lady was controlled by the forces which all young female blacks are exposed to today:

1. She liked getting her freak on which assisted her with creating a fantasy world of illusion in which she failed to cope with life while living in a self created world of partial fulfillment.

2. She ran away at the slightest hint of social pressure – She did not want to cope.

3. She derived pleasure from arguing and working with a black male bozo because she felt smarter than he.

4. She did not like be told what to do – This was her way of rebelling against authority.

5. She had 6-7 different personalities – Jokingly she was called: Sybil

6. The Sybil personalities:

    a. Marie-a loving person who was weak vulnerable and very nice

    b. The Street Girl who was deadly ruthless and mean

    c. Sybil – A woman who you could not cross. If you crossed her it was at your own peril.

    d. The Girlfriend who could be any and everything that a man wanted but who was afraid to let go of her other Sybil like personalities.

Other Observations About Freak Woman:

1. Her brother(s) had been in and out of jail since they were juveniles and they constantly used drugs. They like all of her family members calling upon her for help and assistance.

2. Her mother was an avid user of drugs and alcohol and she was an admitted alcoholic who ruled her family with an iron fist. Freak woman on the other hand tried her best not to be like her mother but in the end all efforts to provide her with assistance failed. Like most twisted sisters she let her bad side control her. In the end, I came to the conclusion that Freak woman was a bad investment that there

was nothing more that I could do to assist her with her problem of twisted ness; She loved her lifestyle and like most twisted sisters she was not going to change it until fate intervened. It is most important that parents understand that you should do your best to keep your children from all drugs especially rock cocaine. This is a special message to you: Please remember that once your children use these mind altering drugs that you will never get them back. They belong to the "rock man". And even if by some strange miracle that you are reunited with them they will never be the same again. This is a quote from a twisted sister named precious; of course we all know that this is not her real name but she told me that: she used rock she had developed the greatest feeling of extreme gratification and that she felt that she could conquer the world; Later on, when she had hit rock bottom and had be relegated to eating dookie burgers; she now started to realized that she had been regulated and abused by the most divisive drug that the black community has ever seen. It is high time, that all blacks do whatever we can to get this cancer and all drugs out of our community. Because anything that interferes with a black person's ability to thing and to comprehend is not necessary for the stable production and inner growth of our community and the welfare, growth and development of our children.

Chapter 6

LADY J

A sister who pretends to be a lady and she is not one. She manipulates men based on her use of the myth of being a good woman and a user. There is a little bit of lady J in every woman but the problem becomes insurmountable when lady J tries to hurt innocent people. The problem with most sisters is that they do not handle rejection very well. The old saying that a woman scorned is applicable here. Once a sister is betrayed it takes her a long time to get over it. This is a very necessary and sufficient corollary of life. It is hard for sisters to get over pain cause of the following reasons:

1. They believe in getting even

2. The need to punish someone for the wrong done to them is necessary and sufficient for their mental and psychological development.

3. Revenge is something that is best served cold and is a vital and stabilizing element of their relational development

4. I want my man to pay for what he did to me. He has inflicted pain upon me and now I want to inflict double or triple the pain on him.

One consequential observation that I have noticed is the following: The twisted sisters have a tendency to show no mercy with a man whom they consider weak and they will destroy him if he lets them. They have a committed desire to accomplish the following against a weak man:

1. They will lie to him about everything and anything.

2. Committing deeds of dishonesty and verbal abuse are common by them.

3. A twisted sister will tell a man that she loves him and behind his back will sleep with and have relations with friends and foe alike who have nothing going for them other than a short and long trip to jail or a mental institution.

Throughout the writing of this book, a necessary and sufficient notion keeps popping up in my head: what is wrong with these twisted sisters and African Queens; don't they know that they are destroying our own families and race? Another question that can now be posed: is do they even care? I believe that they do not care because as long as they can get what they want and what they need; they the twisted sisters have no intention of doing what is right in their lives; whether it be for them; their families and or offspring.

Chapter 7

THE CHURCH LADIES

These are the great social ladies of the church. These sisters pretend that they are spiritual in nature when they are not. They work the minister of the church and some of them are there for his every whim and adulation. I have known sisters who will do everything that the minister wants them to do. I remember a minister telling me one time that every sister wants a preacher. This particular preacher lost his wife to another guy and he was very bitter against it. What is the role of the church lady in the church?

1. To comfort the minister – Sometimes this calls for more extra curriculum duties than his wife is performing.

2. To date as many brothers and deacons as she can – This enables her to gain power within the church

3. To dress nice and be fashionable-her goal is to attract as many men from the church to her as she can.

4. To be phony and deceptive at the same time

5. To serve the needs of the pastor and the church power structure

6. To live a double life

7. Twisted Church Ladies use religion as a tool to destroy their man and the family unit as we know it.

The old adage of the wolf in sheep clothing is appropriate here. The twisted sister has now become a predator and she destroys anything in her way and uses it for food; this is a sad commentary in that the food that she eats is necessary and sufficient for her own survival. It is an established fact that during slavery religion was an established element for up to freedom; our deliverance from slavery is now a part of a twisted sister dilemma: the pain and frustration of this pronouncement is that these twisted sisters are being used to destroy the black race as a unit as we once knew it. The church ladies are creating havoc in the church in the following manner:

1. They date the preachers and have sexual encounters with them

2. They try to turn the ministers inside and out by making them freaks too

3. They have no shame in taking another woman's boyfriend and or husband.

4. They are cunning and conniving women who use the bible to distort and rule in a relationship.

Chapter 8

THE EDUCATED AND CORPORATE PROSTITUTE

These are the women of business and leisure who will do anything to get what they want to gain power. These are women who will use sex to gain their education and sex to be competitive on the corporate work place. Where are their main goals and objectives?

1. The use the theory that the ends justify the means is appropriate here

2. Sex is seen as a bargaining chip for advancement in life and the corporation

3. To love chucky baby on the job

4. Form coalitions with white females and males on the job to create an illusion and myth of success.

David Halberstram, in his book, **the best and the brightest**, discusses the Vietnam War and how America was supposed to win it with its best and brightest individuals. In essence, according Halberstram we lost the war. I see the same things happening to the black race. Our women in the educated and corporate world are selling brothers out and themselves short. There are so many reasons which can be given to explain this, but for all practical purposes within this particular book, I shall attempt to explain and identify a few:

1. Black corporate and educated twisted sisters want to be like their white counterparts females.

2. They believe that the white male loves them and that they can manipulate him better than a black male; a corollary of this notion is that some of the twisted sisters will use the white male relationship as a revenge device tool to punish the black male who used and abused them

3. The have **"low self esteem"** and hanging and associating with their white counter parts creates within them a feeling of experiencing complete pleasure and ecstasy in their realizing that their accomplishments are being totally accepted.

4. They use sex as a tremendous weapon for implementation of a bargaining chip to get what they want; whenever they want it or need it

Chapter 9

YELLOW SISTERS VS. CHOCOLATE

The female feud that could destroy the black family all together. The notion of the yellow or light skinned sister has always been a part of our cultural heritage and it has constantly been a part of our lifestyle. What is the role of the yellow and or light complexion sisters? Their role can be defined as:

1. To secure because of their color as many white and blacks males in society who give preferential treatment in their daily life styles as they can

2. To under cut and undermine the positive attitudes of positive chocolate sisters.

3. Provide detrimental control attitudes attacks against the dark skinned brother to manipulate him cause he is weak

4. To perpetuate the elemental creation of a mating policy that will keep the birth rates of light skinned blacks in the race constant.

5. The creative continuation of the myth that whiter is better than our dark African heritage.

Yellow sisters have always felt that they are the cream of the crop when it comes to getting all of the attention among black females. She, the yellow sister is cunning, cold and collective. The chocolate sister by contrast is mean, nasty, selfish and brutish. She is hostile and quick to anger. She is twisted because she likes to play the role of the man in the relationship. This type of sister is never happy with the way that life is treating her. She constantly complains and she wants what the Jones has. This type of sister can be very difficult to deal with because she is never happy with the hand and the role that life has dealt her with.

The main problem with the yellow and the chocolate females in the black community is that they have no shame in the way that they try to manipulate and use their black male counterparts; and they are a detriment to our race because they are always fighting and competing. It is amazing how yellow sisters in the East and West coast try to become blacker and they are sensitive of their light complexion skin; while on the other hand the chocolate and light skinned sisters in the South try to use their fair skin ness as superiority too. It is time for the sisters to wake up and become confronted with the realization that we all need to assist each other with the survival movement of the black race. Sisters need to get a serious wake up call and start to understand that unless we all work together that we will perish together. The games of jealously, envy and lust for power and control along with manipulation of the black male species must end.

What Lays A Head For The Yellow And Darked Skinned Sister?

1. More continued proliferation of the black female species as a whole if sisters do not start loving each other and respecting their man better.

2. Complete destruction of the black race as a whole will occur because black females are no longer interested in becoming the strong morale fiber African Queens as we once knew them.

3. This ultimate fighting and bickering on the parts of the black females will lead to a unisex relationship status among females in which the black male will no longer be needed to assist them with becoming real fulfilled women.

4. The sister's role as a positive female model for her offspring will diminish.

5. A large number of black females will become lonely and unhappy females with a high degree efficacy in which they will feel that they cannot make an impact in society.

6. Black females will use any and everything to get what they wants as well as trying to obtain what they need; in essence they will become mean, selfish, self centered and incorrigible females who have no more fiber and structure.

A Promise Of Things To Come:

The ability of the black female to be a co-leader in the development of the family will cause the race to suffer severely and maybe have a complete nervous breakdown. It is almost as if a war of the worlds have started and the causalities of the war will be black females, their loss of dignity; black children with no direction and open hostility against black males will create a rules and regulations violations which will led to the loss of black children's innocence. As for the black males: they will suffer losses of self esteem within their inner souls which will create a serious void in black male leadership in the sub community. The task now before us is that we must now attempt to reverse these actions as we try to create more constructive and positive group to turn back the hands of time. Whether or not we have the stamina or ability to accomplish this; we as a group must channel and summons all of our sense of decency and self respect to do this. Or as an alternative, we run the risk to be totally destroyed as a race; This I promise you will naturally be the end of our proud race as we once knew it.

Chapter 10

YOUNG MOMMAS VS OLD MOMMAS

The young apples falling off the tree verse the old dead apples that wither and die is appropriate here. There has always been a problem with the way that young women try to emulate what their mothers do; mothers and daughters been involved in the shaping of the daughter moral values and fibers in the way that she deals with society and the way that sisters deal with brothers. Who are the young Mommas? The young Mommas can be defined as young ladies between the ages of 14-21; they believe that they have youth on their side and are under the false impression that all men want to love and worship them. They have developed a sense of immaturity which makes them twisted. This is a sad observation considering the fact that they have not lived life long enough to know what life is really all about. They have no sense what it really takes to survive within this complicated world.

Who Are The Old Mommas?
The old mommas are twisted black females from the ages of 35 and up who try to give advice to the young mommas. It is sad to see the old Mommas try to give advice to the young Mommas. What are these old mommas telling the young mommas?

1. Make the man pay for your company and services

2. You are a pretty young thing and he wants you and need you to be whole and fulfilled as a man

3. He is a meal ticket and the savior of the family we can all use him

This creates a strange dilemma for the young mommas because they become confused in developing and shaping their relationships with men. The old mommas have polluted the young girls mind with the negatives that they had against men who they feel did not give them their fair share of success in the relationship; therefore she perpetuates the assertion:

such as all black males are no good. This is further from the truth because all men are not the same. Some are good and some are bad. The mother must allow the young mommas to make their own decisions and mistakes but she the old Momma has a right to provide good moral conscience advice.

Chapter 11

THE PLASTIC SISTERS

Plastic Sisters are the sisters who are fake and plastic in the way that they deal with brothers. These sisters have a unique ability to use and abuse good men by hardening their souls and attitudes towards positive men who want to do great things in society.

Who Are The Plastic Sisters?

The plastic sisters are fake and counterfeit sisters. They have a high degree of being bonk- which simply means that they are going no where in society. What makes the plastic sisters so difficult to deal with?

1. She has no comprehension and or attitude of what being real is all about.

2. Everything about her personality is fake.

3. She always seems to have the truth elude her; she misses the boat because she does not pay attention- because she is a very self centered person.

4. She enjoys dealing with plastic men and other plastic people

5. Plastic sisters smile when they do not want to smile.

6. She enjoys being an actor at her best

7. She lives in a world of fantasy and systematic illusion

8. Finally, the plastic sister's depth perception of what is real in life is distorted. The problem with plastic sisters is that they really do not mean to be the way that there are; but it becomes a problem with the way that there low self esteem is enter acting with their need to try to be for real. It is very difficult for women to try to be for real when they know that they are hurting.

Chapter 12

SISTERS WHO LOVE THE BENJAMINS OVER THE MAN

The basis premise of this chapter is that it deals with sisters who want to take as much money; as they can from a man to clock him from all of his money sources. Their primary concerns in dealing with a brother are:

1. To collect as much money from him as they can.

2. The creative degeneration of a black male to make him earn as much money as he can to assist the black female with obtaining two necessary and sufficient objectives:

   a. To gain what she really wants.

   b. To attain what she needs.

Sisters who love the Benjamin's love to use their man to produce for them "opportunities" to make lots of money. The specific goals and objectives of these twisted sisters are to:

1. Get as much money as they can.

2. Have a male counterpart pay their rent, house note and car notes.

3. Buy her clothes and keep her beautiful and fashionable.

4. Continue her consistent search for a sugar daddy-which will be her golden goose.

5. She wants a man as long as he has money; when he no longer can pay for her luxury needs; she finds another man with more money.

Chapter 13

WHAT IS A GOOD SISTER TO DO?

There are a voluminous number of good sisters within the black race but we have a logistical problem when we start at attempting to discuss them. The antics and charades of the drama queen sisters; young and old have created a morality and community vacuum among the good sisters who want to reclaim their man and their families; against the bozo sisters who do not want to do anything to assist the black community with developing more positive relations between them and their man.

More Observations

I believe that the good sisters are going to have to take full control of their race by telling brothers that there is some genuine value in being honest and upfront in a relationship. All black men are not looking for a woman with a bad attitude and bozo behavior development. This is a call to action for, all the twisted sisters I want them to know that there are some honest and decent brothers who are looking for sisters to be honest, too.

What Must A Good Sister Do To Get A Good Man?

The good sister must understand that she needs to develop complete trust with her man. The trust that a man and a woman needs for developing a positive relationship must be based upon the following:

1. A good sister must go into every relationship by being open and upfront about what she really wants? And what she really needs? She must not lead the man into guessing and trying to read her mind.

2. There can be no lies and manipulation on the part of each individual in their developmental relationship-There can only be one man and one woman in a positive relationship.

3. Each person must bring something positive to the relationship and to the table and leave their negative baggage and drama behind.

Chapter 14

TWISTED BROTHERS DEFINED

Twisted brothers can be defined as black males who have lived a topsy turvy life in which they do not know good people from bad one. A lot of their problems stems from the fact that they have lived a lot of their life listening to the wrong persons and they therefore are put into a position whereby they constantly make mistakes. In my life time, I have met a lot of twisted brothers. Some examples, of twisted brothers are:

Brother Tee Do

Brother Tee Do was a southern radio DJ with a talk show who had a deep rooted hatred for black females; he himself was a closet homosexual and a down low brother long before down low brothers became known. He smoked "pot" a lot and you never knew whether it was his mind speaking or the drugs that he was using. He liked dealing with the dirt; he constantly sought any and all information on others and it never matter to him whether his facts were accurate or not. He was the great deception before it ever happened.

Roscoe

Roscoe was your ideal mans man. He would sell out his own mother down the river if he had to do. As a man, Roscoe was weak and he had low self esteem, he was always trying to copy some one else's idea because he did not feel confident in the way that he did things. In reality, Roscoe was a man who could not function properly unless he had someone else to support him.

The Beast

The Beast was the mad hatter. His father was a junkie and his brother was a junkie. The Beast was a man who had it all; he worked for a government agency and he had a good job with a major company. When did things began to fall for The Beast. The Beast's life started to unravel when he started to have relationships with crack head mommas; this is a sad commentary on his part because it was not long before the women that he dated that used drugs started to get beast hooked. One initial point which led to his downfall; started when he was dating a stripper and he was robbed of a large sum of money in a motel room whereby she had set him up with three robbers; the guys felt sorry for him so they allowed him to have sex with her while they watched. This was the start and initial downfall of him as a strong brother.

Suave'

Suave had a lot of low self esteem-he was a high yellow brother with a weight problem. The death of his mother left Suave vulnerable. He father was an alcoholic whom he saw beat his mother as a child he never forgot that; later on when his father got old and started to repent he was there for him. Suave was never the same after the woman that he loved jerked him around and he started becoming a cross dresser. Later on he married a young lady Sheridan who was a former airline stewardess. Sheridan had problems because she used to date a guy by the name of Terry who used to beat her and broke her arm in several places. Suave was later on dumped by Sheridan and he went on to become a street minister.

Donnie Boy

Donnie Boy was never the same after his wife kicked him out after a nasty divorce and told him that she wanted him to continue to pay on her house note. He was told by his ex never to come to her house without calling first. Donny Boy started to date older women and he manipulated them for fiscal and monetary purposes. The ladies who were of an older nature just wanted companionship; but twisted Donny Boy was fully aware of this-but he continued to use them anyway. Later on Donnie Boy started to started dating women in their late 20's and 30's. These women he would pay for their services. His main request from these ladies was that he wanted them to wash and massage his dirty feet for $30-$40 dollars. But this is when pay back started for Donnie Boy; instead of being the one who manipulated, the young sisters turn him inside out and manipulated him. The notion can be fully advanced that they got paid. Donnie Boy also had low self esteem when it came to dealing with sisters. I believed that some where along the way that Donnie Boy got lost in his dealing relationships with sisters.

James – The man who loved Bonnie

James was a brother who worked for the railroad. He married a woman named Bonnie who was very manipulating and she used his to the max. Bonnie was the kind of woman who had a major domination effect on him. James was a weak brother with no sense of direction and substance. It is interesting to note that when a lady finds that a brother is slow and has no self esteem; that they will manipulate him to an extent whereby he is rendered useless for life. This is what happened to James. He became what you call a "Black Male Automaton" a mindless, spineless and deficient male who is of no use to the black sub community because his whole life is over.

Freaky Dee Kee – The Social Work Fraud

Freaky Dee Kee was a professional social worker who taught social work at a black university and several white ones. He finally that had turned himself into a black white person. Freaky Dee Kee was in loved with white females whom he lived with but Freaky Dee Kee who was a very dark skinned brother had a secret passion for sisters. Freaky Dee Kee would give all of his money to Lady V his live in wife but behind her back he would chase and mate with sisters. His secret love was a lady named Margaret B. later on she who was a teaser of black men was eventually raped by an African Male from Nigeria. Margaret B was to get her MSW degree. She developed several serious relationship problems and had a hatred for men. Margaret B was typical of a lot of sisters who have serious personalities flaws in the way that they deal and interact with brothers.

Robbie – The Player

Robbie was a professional teacher at a Midwestern college. He was a ladies man who loves to be a player his one weakness was that he loved women and he loved playing them. Robbie, a yellow brother himself had a harem of sisters: yellow, black, brown or white; he had access to them all. I guess he was the ultimate players' player. His playing days came to an end when his soon to be ex wife waited for him to come home one night and waited until he went to sleep and got her butcher knife and grabbed his magic wand and told him that if he moved that she was going to cut off all what all the other women wanted; he begged her for mercy and he told her how much he loved her; She believed him fully so she dropped her knife. When she dropped the knife, he knocked her with a right fist and ran into his baby son's room and immediately locked the door. Later on he stated that he knew that that crazy sister would not come in the room and hurt her own child. Sixty days later there were divorced. Rob later on married a college cheer leader and exercise specialist who liked women just as much as he did. To the best of my knowledge they are still married.

Aldophus – King Bozo

Aldophus was a large man who stayed in and out of jail. His one rise to fame was that he loved sleeping with women and their lady relatives whom he would beat up. He did not believe in paying child support and he was a very violent man. I remember watching him work in the produce department of Leonard's Grocery Store; he was ashamed when a guy named Troy and I saw him. I became shocked at seeing the mighty **Aldophus** run from the fear of embarrassment; I can still vividly hear the produce manger calling **Aldophus**! **Aldophus**! come back . But the mighty **Aldophus** just kept running for his life.

Stretch – The baby Factory Maker

Stretch was a black man who loved both white and black women. He was a strange case in that he had 9-12 babies for different sisters and he did not like to pay child support. The strange oddity about Stretch is that he had no babies for the white females that he dealt with. Stretch had a hard time holding a job and like most black men he had a serious love affair with his alleged sexual prowess with women. Stretch was an average looking fellow with a vivid imagination.

Fat Man – I love my white wife

Fat Man was a huge brother who loved sausage and soul food. He was married to a white female. He would do anything to keep his wife happy.

Tobias – The baby making Stud

Toby was a baby factory maker. He had no responsibility and commitment to life like most people his young age was that he wanted to make children and not properly take care of them. He wanted the grandparents to raise his children.

Dogman – A dumb Con Artist

Dogman was a weasel and a loser who had no respect for the mother who raised him. The guy was raised with every opportunity to become successful in life. I am amazed how he chose to waste everything he took was shacking up with a loser white female.

Cletus – I who am smarter than everyone else

Cletus was a typical young man who was trained in the Navy and he came from a good family. His main claim to fame is that he wanted to be a player and a follower his actions ultimately led him to a life of one losing situation after another.

Handyman – The grandfather con artist

Handyman was a King of The losers. He was a dishonest individual who did not have a decent bone in his body. Handyman ruined his wife and his whole family. Handyman was a man who had lived a wasted and twisted life. His whole life was based upon deceit and deception. He did not have a decent bone in his body. Handyman came from a family whereby his mother taught her boys how to be criminals. He went to college and flunked out his first year. His brother Morris had been to reform school several times. Handyman and his whole family had been losers from the start. Handyman had more chances than most people in life. He had the love of a good woman whom he abused both mentally and physically to the max. He tried to burn both his wife and his children in a fire. He loved to play with guns and he had a terrific fondness for weapons; while he himself was a coward and a shadow of a real man.

Chapter 15

BROTHER TEE DO

Brother Tee DO as he was called by his Muslim brothers considered himself to be the messenger. This self described definition on his part did not describe how he really was. Tee DO was a manipulative scary man who loved to live with gossip and innuendo. When things did not work the way that he wanted them to be he would create distortion.

What Was The Main Problem With Brother Tee Do?

1. Brother Tee Do was a turn coat brother who trusted no one and used propaganda means towards anyone whom he did not like.

2. He was a closet down low brother who took pure pleasure out of lying to black females.

3. He hated being black-that is why he dated white females because he had a serious inferiority complex about being black.

4. Like all black males with low self esteem; he felt that he owed his very existence to white society.

5. He is the product of a divorce which may have contributed to his feeling of loneliness and hatred of black females.

6. He had a pure hatred of being black but yet he knew deep down inside that he would never be fully accepted by the white society of which he wanted to be a part of so much.

7. He dated white professional females in abundance and yet they did not give him complete fulfillment either. Most of the white females that he dated felt that he was a plastic black man. They considered him to have no directions and feelings.

8. He was both a Mystery and a Baptist at the same time.

9. He used drugs frequently which may have contributed to his twisted mind.

The basis problem with Tee Do is that he was a Big Little man. He had an enormous problem of low self esteem and he tried to bottle it in a fantasy world that was created by him and for him to totally escape from life's realities namely that of being a real black and strong man. This was something that he really strived for but that in his heart that he knew that he could never achieve because he was a weak and spineless little man who could never be real. He had a serious identity problem with who he was and where he wanted to go. He was a mean and vicious man who had no respect for life and people. Brother Tee Do hated women and he would use every opportunity that he had to discredit them. He had a mischievous element to himself that he believed and creating rumors and mistruths about sisters that he did not like. His main goal in life was a continuous and well orchestrated attack on black females. Tee DO was very unhappy in life and he wanted others to share in his misery. Several sisters were knowledgeable of the fact that he hated sisters. They could not understand his rationale for this belief that but most of the sisters who know him contended that:

1. Tee Do hated all women especially sisters.

2. Tee Do had emotional sexual and instability problems with black females

3. They felt that he was in cable of loving any female because of his homosexual tendencies.

4. Tee Do had some secret lifestyles which interfered and conflicted with what he really wanted be in life. A man who just wanted to be a homosexual down load brother.

5. Tee Do was somewhat you would really call in life as a closet puppy who really wanted to come out but was ashamed to be what he really wanted to be because it conflicted with his professional life.

Chapter 16

BOO BOO

Boo Boo once told me once that his whole life ended the moment that his marriage did not work. I really did not understand that but from that moment on everything was downhill for him.

Who Is Boo Boo?

Boo Boo was a brother from a southern town. He started life as a musician and he was always a good one. But Boo Boo had one projected weakness which a lot of black man has: namely he listens to what others said about him. It was important to him that people said positive things about him because he had a low level of self esteem. But the moment someone said anything bad about him Boo Boo entered in to a verbal tirade against them about things that were rumors and innuendos with no truth or substance about them. It is interesting to note that Roscoe's behavior is typical of a lot of angry brothers who hold the world accountable for things in their lives not being the way that they want them to be.

Boo Boo's Profile

1. All sisters were sluts and whores except his mother and sisters.

2. In order to be a full man; he had to lie to all women and other people.

3. He knew that he was a weak and a spineless little man

4. He considered himself smarter than other people

5. He liked to use lies and deception as tool of communication.

6. He felt that the black man was inferior to whites.

7. He did not like to pay bills

8. Boo Boo was a professional moocher; mooching off friends and family a like with no shame.

9. He loved chasing other men's women and he had no morals and values for the way that he deals with people in life.

10. He believed in getting even.

The whole problem with Boo Boo and brothers who followed his philosophy of life is that the had no respect for women and themselves; thereby they created a situation in which they are useless for themselves and or our black race.

Chapter 17

THE WHITE SHADOW: WILL B

Will B was the white shadow-a man who always wanted to be white and who hated his black yellow skin.

Who Is Will B?

Will B was born in a small southern town and he was a very light skinned brother who was taught from Day one by his grandfather who was a farmer that he was superior to other blacks. In essence, Will B felt that he was white and he always wanted to be white. He went to an all black college and upon graduation he took a job in the western part of the United States. Will B married a white female from the Midwestern part of the United States. Later on, she was to divorce him because she thought that she was marrying a black man but in the end she found out that she was married to a black man in body who was nothing more than a white man himself. Another reason that she left him was that her family told her that if she would divorce him that she could get her family inheritance back. Later on Will B quit his banking job and he went into high school teaching Hispanics and Indians in the western part of the United States. Later on he married a robust Japanese woman and he has not been heard of since.

What Was Will B Twisted Problems?

Will B twisted problems revolved around these:

1. He did not like being black.

2. He feels insecure about his blackness

3. He hated black women; especially all dark skinned sisters and brothers.

4. He loved to make fun of all black people because he did not know who he was and where he fit in the grand scheme of things.

5. He hated his own family who give him his black heritage

6. He considered himself a complete failure

All of Will B problems contributed to his not being able to have a fulfilled relationship with sisters because he knew that he was a plastic brother and a bonk brother who had no intentions of ever being a real person. Brother Will B was a unique twisted brother in that he was plastic, phony, cosmetic and insecure at the same time.

Chapter 18

BROTHERS WHO WOULD BE KING

One of the greatest problems that we have in our communities is the brothers who want to be king. These are your educated brothers and successful brothers in the black sub community who feel that they have an air of superiority over the other brothers and black females in the community. What are some of the traits of the twisted brothers who want to be king?

1. I worked hard for what I got in Life – They believed that no one assisted them

2. I am blessed – Like good things happened by accident or they ordained with hard work and commitment involved.

3. Things come easy for me – I am king

4. The world is mine and I control everything

5. People exist to serve my every whim and desires.

6. All of my needs come first before everyone else.

What Is It That Makes Brothers Want To Become Kings?

It is not difficult to ascertain why a brother who is twisted would want to be a king:

1. This twisted type of brother wants full and immediate control everything in his society.

2. He wants to control his woman and his family too.

3. Everything that he owns and all of yours is his too

4. There is no room for compassion and understanding in his world.

5. He rules all of his relationships and his interactions with others with a selfish hand.

6. He is sarcastic and obnoxious and he loves no one but himself.

7. He perpetuates a life of acrimoniousness in which he liked to engage in combat and control all of his subjects whether they are loyal or not.

Chapter 19

HIP HOP VS GANGSTER THUG

Hip Hop and Gangster Thugs who have manipulated and contorted our twisted sisters and convinced them to committed to the same life style situation which has confused our young.

Who Are The Twisted Hip Hop And Gangster Thugs?

The hip hop and gangster thugs are the new element of the black twisted brothers who are destroying and complicating our race due to their insensitivies of what the beautiful culture of our race is all about. **How are they accomplishing this?**

1. They picture all black females who are our African queens as bitches and whores.

2. Their music glorifies a negative weak and bozo type black male as a strong and glorified individual.

3. All black women are characterized as weak minded submissive females who will do anything for the black if he dogs, uses dishonesty tactics, and disrespects her.

4. In their whole sub culture black males and are characterized as cave men and women with brains the size of a pea.

5. In their world both the woman and the man are pictured as useless and unnecessary to the survival of the world as a group

6. All the blacks in this culture are portrayed as glorified users and abusers of society who constantly use violence, bozoism and disrespect for the system as a way to be successful in society.

Chapter 20

THE PERFECT BROTHER

These are the brothers who feel that they have got it made and that they are different from the loser brothers. We can all agree that there is no such person but we can give some attention to it for illustrative purposes. There is no such notion as a perfect brother in real society because life is a continuing series of people who are striving for perfection but in the twisted world of black males there is a segment of black bozo who feels that they are perfect for the following reasons:

1. They feel that they are far more superior in intellect to the dumb brothers

2. No one can tell them anything because they know everything

3. They have an incorrigible ability to feel that no one can teach them anything; they believe that their way is the best alternative in the way that they deal with life.

4. They are incorrigible in the way that they view and perceive life.

5. They are willing to destroy everything in order to perceive what they feel is necessary and sufficient to gain what they want and what they really need.

6. They are very difficult people to deal with.

7. They have developed an attitude of being very mysterious in the way that they conduct personal and business relationships with others.

8. They are not willing to share their ideas with people whom they mistrust and or are afraid of.

9. They have lived sheltered lives and they have an abundance of low self esteem.

There future is bleak considering the notion that they are reluctant to change. They have an inherent belief that life belongs to them and that they ought to live it to the fullest with no interruptions are positive advice from individuals who know the system inside and out. They are very rebellious and they hate all authority figures or any one who can bring some type of stability to their lives. In a recalcitrant way, they want to remain in the dark and lost from all the beautiful advantages that life has to offer.

Chapter 21

BROTHER FREAKY DEE KEE – THE MAN WHO LOVED WHITE FEMALES

I first, met Freaky Dee Kee in 1978, Freaky Dee Kee was from Chicago and he was a professor at a Midwestern Black University, David had a problem with being black. He was a dark skinned brother. David had a live in wife who was also a faculty member from Omaha Nebraska. Her name was Lady X. She loved her some Freaky Dee Kee and Freaky Dee Kee loved him some Lady X. Lady X and Freaky Dee Kee had a strange relationship: She loved the young male students and He loved the young black female students. Freaky Dee Kee dated several black female students in his classes but he would never give up Lady X. He loved her and he cared for her very much to the extent that he was a black white man who did not believe that he was black. I tend to believe that Freaky Dee Kee had been brainwashed as a child that white was better. It is sad to see how twisted he was in that all that Lady X had to do was whistle and Freaky Dee Kee would come running like a puppy. It is ironic that even when Freaky Dee Kee cheated on Lady X that he felt guilty. All Lady X had to do was just confront him and Freaky Dee Kee would whim like a fully contented puppy.

The Tipster And Lady I

Freaky Dee Kee's partner in crime and ace boon coon was a brother by the name of Tip. Tip was also married to a white female. Her name was Lady I and she were from South Dakota. Tip had a tremendous weakness for the white female because she provided him with security. The factor which made Tip twisted was that he loved to have a sister on the side because it made him feel less guilty. Tip knew in his heart that he could not have a productive relationship with a sister. There is an old saying in the black community by sisters which state that once a black man loves a white female that he is ruined for life. Such was the case with both Freaky Dee Kee and Tip both of these brothers because of their relationships with white females were damaged for life and that they could never in

65

a real sense have a productive relationship with a sister because they would always have the memories of their previous relationship with the white females.

Chapter 22

MR. ROBINSON

Mr. Robinson is the husband who cheats on his wife. What are some of the reasons that a black man gives for cheating on his wife:

1. He feels guilty

2. The Brother feels that he is both sexually and mentally incompetent

3. He feels that he does not make enough money

4. He cannot handle the pressure of life.

5. The ego of the black male is too fragile

6. He cannot measure up

7. The failure of the black female to understand his problems

8. He is a Mandingo sexual warrior

9. She is a player too

10. He cannot open up to all her demands and drama

11. She is there to be his slave and puppet

12. She is not smart enough for him

13. She is a loser as a potential mate

14. He disrespects his woman and he feels that she is too weak as a person to provide him with the totally peace of mind which he constantly seeks

15. There is more to his life than dealing with his mate because life has so much more to offer.

These types are brothers are not real good role models because both the male and female offspring will have a tendency to feel that their father has neglected them and he has no intentions of keeping the family together.

Chapter 23

YELLOW BROTHERS
VS.
DARK MANDINGO BROTHERS

There has always been a problem in relationship communication and understanding between dark skinned and yellow skinned brothers. This is easy to understand why these two types of brothers do not like each other for the following reasons:

1. The yellow brother feels that he is superior to the black brothers.

2. Yellow brothers think that they are white

3. Yellow brothers feel that they are pretty boys.

4. Dark brothers feel that they are stronger and manly than yellow brothers.

5. Dark skinned brothers feel that they are sexually superior to yellow brothers

6. Dark skinned brothers feel that they are more macho than yellow skinned brothers.

7. Both dark skinned and yellow skinned brother's bozo tendencies.

8. The dark brothers like to fight and they are quick to anger and violence

9. Yellow Skinned brothers feel that they have an advantage over the dark skinned brothers because white society accepts them more.

10. Dark Skinned Brothers feel left out of the systematic process because of their skin color so they try to compensate by being more violent and hostile in the way that they deal and comprehend relationships with others.

Chapter 24

TWISTED SISTERS AND DUMB BROTHERS: THE MAKING OF BABY ZOES

One of the biggest problems that are leading to the destruction of the black race is the creation of Baby Zoes. Bozo men and women who mate together create Baby Zoë children. This is sad to see because it is not the choice of the baby offspring. They did not ask to come into this world but rather it is the job of Mommy and Papa to educate train them and to provide them with the proper survival skills.

How Are Baby Zoes Created?

Baby Zoes are created when male and female Zoes mate together. People have a right to date who they want and to mate with whomever they chose but when it comes to Baby Zoes they are some distinct problems of survival. What are some of these problems?

1. The creation of a Baby Zoë brings a child into a family who may be taught all of the same characteristics that his parents have.

2. Baby Zoë will not have a positive chance to survive in society due to the negative attitudes and experiences that his parents may bring to the table.

3. During the early childhood years of development and growth-Baby Zoë may be taught same negative learning behavior from being exposed to a negative and unproductive environment that his parents may have came from.

4. The frustration and the inner hostilities that the family may have suffered in their past may be transferred to Baby Zoë thus making it impossible for the child to survive.

5. The inner jealously of Mary Zoë and Papa Zoë about the empty feeling of their life going no where may be transferred to Baby Zoë.

6. All mothers love their children but the inner emotional and relationship problems between Momma Zoë and Papa Zoë may be transferred to Baby Zoë thus providing Baby Zoë with a serious feeling of instability and emotional problems with dealing with his or her life.

CONCLUSION

This particular analysis has in a small way tried to analyze what has happened to the great and proud black race as we once knew it. There are several crucial and critical questions which are deemed to be answered here. We now need to bring them to the forefront.

Some Final Thoughts On The Destruction Of The Black Race Process

This analysis has basically tried to provide some interesting insight into why the black race as we once knew it is on its way towards total destruction and annihilation

How Can Blacks Stop Eliminate And Slow Down This Process:

The key to stopping the whole elimination the eradication of the proud black race as we once have known it; is to figure out what are we going to do to pull ourselves out by the bootstraps and get our economic development and moralist acts together in order that we survive instead of perishing together. A necessary and sufficient derivative for understanding this process will be for the black citizen to try to understand two unequivocal points of interests:

1. How To Learn To Respect Each Other

2. How To Learn To Work And Get Along Together

There are no other theoretical concepts of life which makes it harder for blacks to learn more important than that we have to learn to give each other proper respect and the perpetuate the notion that in order for us to prosper that we must learn how to work together.

General Black Systematic Terms

There are several systematic terms which will be utilized throughout the reading of this book. Some of there are:

1. **The Bozo** – A dumb brother who has no respect for his woman and or himself. He uses force to solve everything and he has a pea for his brain.

2. **The Hood** – The boundaries of location in which ghetto blacks feel secure and comfortable.

3. **My Girl** – The feeling of creation by a brother that his woman belongs to him and no one else.

4. **Skirting** – The ability to maneuver with the systematic process without breaking the laws of the systematic process but rather going to the edge of the process without going over.

5. **The Rules of the Game** – These are distinct rules which govern all aspects of the systematic process. The rules are clear and they are to the point. All must obey the rules are they risk facing the wrath of the system.

6. **Dude** – An average black male

7. **That's F.....K Up** – A popular phrase among blacks when things are not going the way that they are supposed to.

8. **Down Low Brothers** – Brothers who love women and men and are very secretive.

9. **Down Low Sisters** – Sisters who love men and women and are very secretive.

10. **The theory of the Mystic** – The underlying element in any systematic relationship which governs the outlook of a relationship. It thrives off of control and mysticism.

11. **G-Money** – A ghetto slang for dope dealers with money.

12. **Player** – A brother who plays around with the game of love.

13. **Playette** – A woman who plays around with the Game of love.

14. **Peer Group** – those who have the power to influence the outcome of the game.

15. **Skizer** – one who tries to use another person too much.

16. **Play Too Many Games Theory** – a systematic game in which there are no winners and losers but the exercise of the Game creates a plus one and a minus one situation; and the game participants cancel each other out.

17. **My Man** – Brothers who love brothers from the hood-they hug each other and show much affection when they meet

There are other systematic terms which will be discussed in a future book. But for purpose of a theoretic framework of this systematic process; these are necessary and sufficient. In this book, the author has tried to take the reader on a wonderful but correct and concise journey to try to understand the black system. There are so many problems which we are confronted with in our daily lives which can be address to and properly dealt with if we had the proper knowledge and a thorough understanding of the black system. This book is a conceptive and constructive attempt to provide the reader with the following:

A Through Understanding Of The Black Relationship Healing Process

- We need to develop and implement a proper theoretical framework for understanding the roles of black females and males in our current black society as it exists today.

- To identify and utilized proven systematic successful problem solving techniques and positive solutions as they relate to blacks in America

- To examine proven systematic cases and their solutions to assist blacks with solving their problems.

- To Educate the Black Male and Sisters on How to respect each other and how to really love one and another. The reality which this book illustrates is that all aspects of positive relations and the goal of a healthy life are to understand each other and work on positive dealings with each other.

James Reedom is a former professor of both Political Science and Public Administration. He has taught his first college level course at the age 22 when all his colleagues were in their late 50's and 60's. He has taught at Universities in New York, Missouri, Louisiana and Texas. He has worked as a director of several non profit organizations, developed college criminal justice programs, business consultant and crisis management counselor just to name a few.

Further Thoughts On This Book 's Message

This book can be of enormous usage to the black males and females who has taken a beating from non productive relationships and disrespect for each other. As I have stated previously that the purpose in writing this book is to assist those who have been abused by the relationship process because some overzealous black male and or female, organization and or systematic institution have taken the little person for granted because they did not totally and or even in a small way understood the concepts and precepts what it really means to be black in America.. I am living proof of and here to day because of all the little people who stood up tall and they used the systematic process to their best advantage. I can still remember both my "mom and Pop" both trying to install in myself and my twelve brothers and sisters on how to learn all that we could because at some point in life that we were going to need them. Little did I know that how right that they were. A key element of this book is that if one learns how to master systematic concepts; they will be more able to handle any problem properly. The knowledge that I have attained over the years has enabled me to utilized full knowledge and understanding of the systematic process. One has to learn that there are only two kinds of people who make it in society. Namely these are:

1. The best liked

2. The Most Competent or Knowledgeable

Most of us blacks border on being the most liked but I have come to the conclusion that if a black person learns all the maximums of the Systematic Process" that one will be able to open doors which never existed to them before such as:

• Learning How To properly deal with each other

• Educating themselves against hating other blacks

- Controlling our tempers against each other

- Being in Total Control of Your Romance and Marriage and dating life

- Controlling animosity on the job

- Minimizing Costs and Maximizing Profits In basic black male and female relationships

- Controlling Black Stress and Emotions

- Learn How to fight the urge to use and manipulate each other.

- Fight male egoism and female superiority

- Saving the home and the family as a structural support unit

- Live a comfortable life Free of Systematic Stress which is a key to destroying black male female relationships

- Becoming More Knowledgeable About The System which will make both the black male and female stronger

- Learn The True Art of Politics in relationships and marriage

- And Much More

The tenets of this book will make your vision of the systematic process much clearer and it will enable the consumer to develop and implement a much keener and open minded sense of what the system is all about. This book my friends will enable each individual who reads it to live and enjoy a much kinder and gentle life. Let the journey begin.

The Systematic Process: As It Relates To Blacks

The systematic process is not a new phenomenon. The system has existed for some time now and it has ruled and have governed all aspects of individual society for quit a while. But the problem which most individual consumers are confronted with is that they do not understand all the concepts about the systematic process. For example, a parent sends their children off to school because we have laws and regulations governing the way that a child ought to be educated. Adults abide by driving laws because we know that if we do not obey traffic regulations that we might end up with a traffic citation and or fine and that if we further do not abide by the rules that we could end up in jail and or pay a fine. If a DAD does not pay for the support of his child; he could find himself in serious trouble and or ultimately be confronted with facing the State in a serious matter. Some systematic theorists throughout the years have tried to keep this knowledge away from the consumer. I state to you that if you learn to master most of these systematic techniques; you will learn to have control of all aspects of your life and that there will be no need to panic anymore. In our effort to learn about the system; Let us begin with a discussion of the following systematic theorists:

1. W.E. Dubois

2. George Washington Carver

3. Fredrick Douglas

4. Alvin Poussaint

5. Malcolm X

6. Muhammad Ali

7. Jacques Eullul: The Political Illusion

8. The Notion of I am Ok and You are not

9. The Crush Syndrome

10. Looking Out For Number One

11. The Ends justify The Means

12. The Panic Syndrome

13. The Copycat Syndrome

14. The Greed Factor

15. Who Get What When And Where

16. The Haves vs. The Have Nots

17. Love vs. Revenge

18. The Concept of Mercy Vs. Get Even

19. Help Is On The Way

    a. The DuBois view of thought discusses how the Blackman show use education as a key to gaining prominence and respectability in life. The notion was expressed that the more educated that the Sraggin became in society the more that he would be able to gain acceptability and prominence. The only problem with this case scenario is that education has not enable the Sraggin to become totally free in essence, he has adopted many of the bad traits and attitudes of his white counterparts.. So much in fact now that we are beginning to wonder where do we go from here?

    b. George Washington Carver's View of life-operated on the premise that The Sraggin should develop skills so that he could make a worth contribution to life and feed his family in order for the Sraggin To survive within the system.. This premise contended that several notion maximums contributed towards the survival of the Sraggin:

        1. Learning a skill

        2. Perfecting Your Skill

    c. The Notions are:

        1. With a skill the Sraggin's Survival was imminent

2. The Sraggin would be more able to feed his family

3. Knowledge of a skill would guarantee's the Sraggin's survival and Contribution to Society.

4. The Sraggin would always be needed.

The key elements in understanding this notion was that they were set up for Sraggin survival

d. **Martin Luther King** – was a civil rights leader who believed in equality for all people.

e. **Malcolm X** – started off hating white people for injustices committed against blacks but later on he found out all men are brothers regardless of their race.

f. **Frederick Douglas** – was a slave who wanted to be free; he eventually ran away and became a pillar of Washingtonian politics..

g. **Alvin Poussant** – In his book Why Blacks kills Blacks deals with the labels which society places on individuals in a direct contrast of social symbolism.

h. **Eullul** – In his book "The Political Illusion" discusses the Individual within society vs. The Myth-which is the underlying element which forces us to believe in our systematic process.

i. **I'm Okay: Your Okay** – This is the systematic process way of justifying your own actions whether legal or illegal. These contentions are based upon the individuals inherent believe that they are right.

j. **The Crush Syndrome** – The systematic Notion that we have to destroy and crush all our enemies.

k. **Looking out For Number One** – This systematic philosophy advocates looking out just for yourself and putting your self before everyone else. I have always believed that this notion is the systematic process at its worst. Simply stated. One cannot survive in an atmosphere of isolationism. There are points in time when you have to depend upon the assistance of others and work with them in a spirit of positive cooperation.

l. **The Ends Justify the Means** – This is another individualistic systematic philosophy whereby an individual sometimes perpetuate wrong deeds and provides self justification for them. For instance, it is wrong for an individual to justify breaking the law simply because they want break the rules.

m. **The Panic Syndrome** – Some systematic cohorts do things based upon the fact that they are prone to panic. In a serious systematic and problem solving situation: there is no time for panicking.

n. **The Copycat Syndrome** – These are people who like copying the ideas of others for profit and personal gain. They are not true systematic cohorts.

o. **The greed factor** – These individuals are driven by their own personal gain and are not in compliance with looking at the true values which life has to offer us.

p. **The Haves and the have-nots** – This philosophy perpetuate the notion of those who have and those who do not: namely the have nots. There is a constant struggle for power between the two groups when they are in the power game of control of the systematic process.

q. **Love vs. Getting Even** – When systematic cohorts is in love with each other; the sky is the limit. But the situation drastically changes when love turns into hate. This changes the nature of the relationship into one of Hate and Revenge.

r. **Who Gets what when and where** – This is the old Harold D. Laswell Book describing how power is dispersed within the systematic process.

s. **The concept of Mercy vs. Getting Even** – This is a strange systematic philosophy because it perpetuates that when someone makes you mad within a systematic struggle that you should show no mercy. Coupled with this philosophy is the inner notion that one must learn how to be benevolent and show compassion and not want to overkill because at some point you may be on the opposite side one day.

t. **Help Is On The Way** – His concept has as its main premise that if you learn how to master the systematic process that you will be able to have Help Is On The Way at all times no matter how the situation might be.

There Are Three Types Of Systematic Problems. These Are:

1. Level I Communication Problems

2. Level II Communication Problems

3. Level III Communicational Problems

Level I

Level I-systematic problems are the highest degree of the systematic process which individuals have to deal with. These types of problems involve the following:

a. Divorce

b. Sexual Abuse

c. Physical Abuse

d. Jealously rages

e. Mental Abuse

f. Children Abuse

g. Divorce when property is at stake

h. Sexual Molestation

i. Child Support

j. Spousal Abuse

k. Deception

l. Deceit

m. Acts of Passion

n. Acts of Hate

o. Murder

Level II Type

This is your middle of the road systematic problem which deal with your every day living.

a. Education and Economic Development Related

b. Problems with your Survival

c. Problem with a spouse or love one

d. Marital Problems

e. Adult Related

f. Child Support

g. Older Parents/Relatives improper treatment

h. Increasing the Quality of Life

i. Systematic Adjustments

j. Small legal-normally of the civil and or small criminal variety

Special Relationship Problems

These are problems which occur when supervisor or significant other or even friend and or close confident refuse to assist you and things have gotten out of hand and there is no one that you can turn to for immediate help. The pressure is mounting up and you seem no options for dealing with the situation.

1. High level managerial positions which lead to your apparent dismissal. You may know too much and you may become a threat to the company and or organization.

2. Being in the wrong place at the wrong time a lot of blacks suffer from this.

3. An accomplished "whistleblower" that has been set up for passed indiscretions-Blacks are notoriously known for telling on each other because they do not like a person or a thing. In certain situations where the statements that they may are not true; they will still try to create distortion.

4. Hostile home and personal relationship situations job situations

5. Special systematic indiscretions Problems-These are problems in which black males and females have critical problems of getting along. These situations create a negative role model for the children and other family members.

6. Female/Male related problems of a violent and a criminal nature.

7. Special Divorce related problems

8. Vengeance and ill reverence related problems

These systematic problems are not inclusive because there are illustrative of some in which the reader can add to the list as a prescriptive framework of conceptual analysis for trying to understand how blacks try to deal to deal with the systematic process.

Temitra Story

Some parts of this story will sound incredible but it is the truth only the names have been changed. Temitra along with three other females were injured in a car accident. She was in a coma and almost dead for a long time. Some how by a miracle of faith she survived but this is where her problems started :

1. Although the adolescents had suffered serious injuries; they were not awarded more than $15,000-$25,000 by the time that they reached 18 years old.

2. All of their parents were Daddy and Mommy Zoe's.

3. The girls before they were eighteen years old they were all pregnant.

4. All the girls started to use drugs and exhibit momma zoe behavior.

5. Temitra started a relationship with a drug dealer. Her romance with him was short lived because he was given 25 years for his drug dealing.

6. Temitra continued to fall through the cracks as her drug use continued and her open hostilities against men continued. She hung around with a bunch of other females whose main goal was to fleece older men out of their money to perpetuate her continued drug use habits. Temitra is parting of a growing breed of young black sisters who have taken a vacation away from society; She does not understand that by taking herself out of society that she has become of a new breed of sisters and brothers appropriately named as the"Living Dead". These are persons who have decided that their have decided that they do not want to be a vibrant and integral part of life. These individuals life for their own selfish desires and needs and they have no intentions of becoming a contributing member of society.

What does the future hold for the Black race given all the problems that we are faced with today?

1. Instant destruction if corrective measures are not taken to save the race. It is important that black understand that if they do not pull together and become one unified group; the prospects for living a good and quality life will become bleak and that they will not have an opportunity to survive as a group. This is hard for some people to understand but they must come to the realization that there is unity in strength. The alternative to unity is disunity and that will lead them to the down ward spirals pitfalls and no one wins. Evidence of this notion existing is provided

to us on a daily basis; we see the selfishness which exists within the black family and social sub cultural systems. It seems as if blacks are openly jealous and envious of each other; the avocation of this notion can do nothing more than destroy our family.

2. Complete need to reconcile all differences- Black males and females have to both realize that unless both species group rectifies their differences that the black race as a whole will not have a chance to survive. The old saying that everyone should do their own thing and use each other to the max is not applicable here. The old adage that a mind is a terrible thing to waste is applicable at this point because it is high time that both males and females with the sub community become fully responsible for their actions. To this point both groups have been deficient in the way that they have been accountable and responsible for their negative actions which have had a detrimental effect on the positive awareness of how the race needs them.

3. The need to create positive role models for all black children-We must find some way if our race is to survive to find positive and constructive ways to give our young children more positive role models with our race. This must be done both by black males and black females. The negative role models out there to day have had nothing but a negative effect upon our children's developmental and responsible growth.

4. The elimination of all negative attitudes between black males and females

5. The Re-emergence of the black males and females as strong moral fiber units within the sub community- It is now time for the black male and the black female to become more responsible individuals within their communities by developing more strong moral values and to try to re-establish God and moral fiber and faith in their lives. We have too many people who are willing to do wrong things because they feel that everybody is doing wrong things; this is the truth because a strong moral fiber builds a strong inner person who is more knowledgeable about a feeling of right and wrong and he strives to live a good, fair and honest life.

6. The Development of Self Empowerment Economic and Community Development Opportunities for low income and moderate opportunities blacks. We have to provide low to moderate income persons with an ample and equal opportunity to survive. This is a very important aspect of thought for the blacks to understand. We must understand that just because a black person is poor is not an excuse for not trying to excel.

7. The perpetuation of Both W.E. Dubois and Booker T. Washington Philosophies of Life-Dubois and Washington both advocated that the Blackman should try to do something in life. We need to re-establish these philosophies of black life; We must understand that both the males and females must understand that the more that we try to do positive things that the more that we will be able to do positive things in the community and become a more positive influence in the community.

8. Black Women Should Reassume their roles as the Matriarch of the families

9. Black Males Should Reassume their roles as the Patriarch of the families-Black males need to re-establish their roles in the families by becoming more of a positive influence in their families. It is time for black males to stop being little boys. Black Men should become more responsible for their actions. The notion of accountable and responsibility must be installed in black men. Your community and your family need you.

10. Establishing the notion that children come first and the needs of Momma and Daddy second- It is very important that we re-establish within the black female and male that notions that the selfish needs of momma and daddy come second compared to the needs of the children. It is the main responsibilities of the parent to provide their kids with love, affections and positive growth development. All black parents should to teach them the positive aspects of life. All parents must learn how to sacrifice their own self needs and go for the positive investment of what is best for the child.

11. Re-establishing their faith in prayer and GOD-GOD should be become the focal point and directional influence of all what is good for black males and females in life. We are going through hard times because we have taken God out of our lives

and are concentrating just on the material things; Even Jesus told us be grateful of the things that God has given to you because when you leave this world you take nothing with you other than the positive good that you earn when you were here.

12. The positive reinforcement among Black males that they are the descendants of African Kings this was a point in history that we as African Queens and Kings were the center of all culture of what was good and best for civilization. Some how or another, we as a race of people have lost this. It is now time that we go back to the basics: we must learn how to utilize the talents and contributions of all of people; We must remember that there is unity in strength. If we do not learn to work together and to assist each other; we will perish.

13. The reestablishment of the notion that race among blacks and whites is still the number one problem in America-Racism in America will not go away. You cannot make a person love you but you can show that person that people who thrive off of hate will not be able to become a functional participant in society. We as a group of people must learn to work within this hate and build a positive sphere of development for ourselves and out communities.

14. Are we our brothers keepers-Yes we are our brothers keepers and we must remember that as long as one brother and sister is left behind; we are all left behind. Each and every one of us must become a committee of one to assist all of our brothers and sisters with becoming more self sufficient.

15. What did Hurricane Katrina-September 2005 Teach Us – It told white and black America the following:- The hurricane tragedy has told America that unless we all learn to live together and try to love, help and assist all men and women with trying to live and survive in American none of us have a chance of living a quality of life in America. The racist attitudes and opinions of some individuals namely the in group has made life difficult for the poor, the sick, the downtrodden and the disadvantaged. It is important that we understand in American that we have to change our vision that I have mine theory and that you can work hard to get yours theory is deficient and unacceptable. This country has survived for years off of the

efforts of the poor and the disadvantaged and we have done nothing to assist these people with getting back on their feet. The greatest prosperity that Americans have always endured has came after we have assisted the poor and the downtrodden and the disadvantaged . It is not a matter of Republican and or Democrat but rather all Americans supporting helping and assisting others. America became great because all Americans black and white, brown and international and Native Americans contributed to the process.

16. What in store for New Orleans? There are hard times in store for New Orleans because New Orleans is a typical urban city with a large number of blacks. What is in store for New Orleans? There is a lot that New Orleans will have to deal with: contrary to popular belief is now an accepted notion that the rebuilding of New Orleans is going to take 5-6 years to rebuild. What are some of the things which are going to have to occur before New Orleans is rebuilt are:

   a. The levees are going to have to be properly rebuilt and are properly designed to properly withstand a category 5, 4 and 3 hurricanes.

   b. Politics in New Orleans and Southern Louisiana will have to undergo a new rebirth period.

   c. Blacks in New Orleans are going to have to be part of the new developmental process.

   d. The bottom Land areas of New Orleans are going to have to be rebuilt and or redevelopment.

   e. Citizens of New Orleans who do not want to come will have to be reimbursed for their losses.

   f. The cultural history of New Orleans must be restored and or preserved.

   g. The Motto so goes New Orleans so goes the country is appropriate here.

   h. The Rebuilding of New Orleans will make it the New Model City of the South.

i. The Rebuilding of New Orleans will make more economic and economic development opportunities available for Blacks.

j. The creating of more job opportunities for low income and moderate citizens.

k. The Gulf Coast region needs to be rebuilt. The rebuilding of the Gulf Coast will create new economic and development opportunities for blacks

l. Blacks needs to become more serious about saving their race and creating a desire and implementation process for participating with the systematic process.

m. Blacks should strive not to just use the political process to seek equality within the system.

n. Blacks as members of the out group need to utilize their training

Further Analysis Of The Twisted Sister And Dumb Brother Dilemma

Blacks are in a very dubious situation whereby all of the positive and substantive gains which has occurred since the 1960's has been overly overturned due to their reluctance to be open and upfront in working for positive development of the race. The situation has gotten completely out of hand because the twisted brothers and sisters have taken complete control over our once proud race as we once knew it. They constantly disrespect us by calling us "old school" instead of respecting us for building all the positive things that we have done for them. As the late comedian Rodney Dangerfield once said: I cannot get any respect.

What Is It That These Twisted Brothers And Sisters Are Now Teaching Their Offspring?

1. They are teaching their offspring to be hostile and angry with all blacks; ill regardless of the situation. It is significant to note that both males and females have passed their acrimonious relationships on to their children and or offspring

2. We all are aware of the fact that children are God's greatest creation and we are not passing some of our greatest positive traits of love, honesty, commitment and caring for and helping one and another; but rather we are passing all of our most negative traits. Like Comedian Bernie Mack has said "Wake up America" I now say: Wake Up Black America.

What Are Some Of The Negative Traits Now Being Passed?

1) The notion that we should teach our kids how to be mean and hostile; So many of the twisted brothers and sisters are teaching their young kids how to be mean and hostile just like them. This type of behavior in the black sub community is unfair and not right; if we are to give our kids the best of what we are as real people. We want to provide our kids with positive motivational traits which will allow them to survive in society not just negative ones. Screaming, fighting and cussing is not proper behavioral if young people are to learn how to survive.

2) Passing on the trait of using any and everybody to get what you want and really need in society; This trait is a very destructive one in that it builds negative character in our youth. It makes a person believe that they cannot accomplish anything in life unless; they the individual uses each and every other person. We need to inform to all of our children and young relatives that no body makes it in life unless some other positive person works with them. Each and every one of us need other positive people to work with us in order that we can become the best person that we want to be and that we can make a worthy commitment to society.

3) Conveying to our children that dishonesty pays off vs. being honest and virtuous and righteous. This is a trait that we need to abolish from our black sub community immediately because it has become a thorn in the side of our people who want to learn how to positively communicate with one another. We have to teach our kids to be fair and honest and upright with each other. We must follow edits of honesty and be virtuous in the way that we conduct out lives and constantly deal with each other. We must teach out young offspring as well as re-orientating ourselves to the values of really loving one and other and taking care of each other.

4) Telling young girls that it is ok to be promiscuous; as long as she gets paid. This is a bad assumption on the parts of family members and individuals who ill advise young people with this nonsensical notion. There is an old adage that you get what you pay for in life seems to be appropriate here; If we teach our children to sell themselves to the highest or lowest bidder; is one of the most serious kinds of moral injustice that we can convey to our kids and that this immoral conveyance creates one of the greatest injustices which can be committed against out young offspring within the sub community. We must teach our children about following the straight and narrow paths of life so that they may be in a more advantageous position to deal with life and all of the positives and unassuming roles and situations that they will have to be confronted with.

5) Exposing young boys to the notion that it is ok to use and abuse and use all our sisters because all women are boppers. This trait is tantamount to a black male considering himself to being a beast of burden and an animal with no brain. All men young and old must learn how to be accountable for each and every one of their actions. The male species must learn how to treat all of his sisters with honor, respect and dignity; this the only way that a black male can learn why his sister is both necessary and sufficient to the family because we are all family; it is this notion of family which is essential to the inner stability and continued growth and structure of our black race as a whole.

This is a sad commentary considering the fact that we all have had and excellent opportunity for blacks to save our race as a whole. It is now, high time for each and every one of us to become a committed of one and Wake Up: Black America To Get back On Track. How are we going to accomplish this. If we are too totally and unequivocally realize this goal. All Blacks must come to grips with the following:

1) Blacks need to become more focused and start to realize that our very own moral fiber and holistic source of cultural understanding with our sub communities has been challenged; that we are lost and are following the yellow brick road of systematic disillusionment. The time for blaming the "white man and society and each other for our failure to communicate and to love one and another is over. Since the 1960's, we have had the opportunity and the power to control our own

destiny but have continued to sit back and watched idly by while others have taken all of the gains which we made through the civil rights movement and have passed us by; we have allowed our own stubborn and negative attitudes to slow us down with a continued dose of systematic self esteem which have dramatically lower our feelings of efficacy about ourselves; now we feel ashamed about ourselves and where we are going we have become like Ralph Ellison in his book the "Invisible Man" has said we are an invisible people we live a live whereby we are not even noticed; not even by ourselves. This has happened to a large extent because we have try to copy too many negative traits of those who are in control and who have the power. This collaboration whether willing or unwillingly has now lead us to abandon our true self and the lost culture which has made us stop loving and caring for each other.

2) Black leaders, ministers, educators, lawyers and successful business persons need to: stop being socialistic pimps and try to lead our people by example instead of using them. They need to be part of the solution instead of contributing to the problem.

3) Young brothers and sisters need to learn all of the communication skills of the system and learn how to properly develop all of their cognitive skills. Learning how to think and properly reason with others will keep a lot of the twisted brothers and sisters out of trouble and jail.

4) Above all we should try to be responsible for all of our actions; because no matter what happens to us in life jail is not an option.

5) "Rap and Hip Hop "music is sending out the wrong subliminal secret coded messages to our children; Their minds are being clouded with mistruths and programming to make them focus on the wrong goals and objectives of life. Both Tupac and Biggie are dead because their subliminal music was sending the wrong signals about the gold and glitter lifestyle which was misplaced and misguided and developed detrimental social values for our sub community.

6) All black men need to become responsible and learn how to take care of their babies and not just leave them to the care of the grandparents

7) Avoid "crack cocaine "and all drugs at all costs because they fry you brain and take away from you the essence of what you really are a good man and a good woman who is something very special: African kings and queens; from the mother country.

8) Both black men and women need to develop strong moral values and fibers within themselves and try to set proper role models for our kids. Believe it or not? Kids are our best assets and investment. If we properly train them ;we will realize that a sound investment in our race's future will occur. The one derivative and constant in this observation is that: we must realize that our children are imitative and they are repetitive in the ways that they emulate our every move. It is important that we give our kids the best that we have to offer; not our worst. These words to the wise are sufficient for all of us to heed. I believe that following them will assist us with helping our children and saving our race.

9) Blacks need to follow the Ten Commandments more and follow the edits and examples of the bible. Some important, observations are:

   a. Honor thy mother and father

   b. Do not covet the Neighbors wife.

   c. Do not bear false witness against thy neighbor

10) Parents and guardians need to do background checks on who their kids are associating with. The world as we know it is constantly in flux; we need to keep positive tabs on our younger people; our goal is to monitor the actions of our kids and make sure that they are not falling into the clutches of manipulative and evil people.

11) Older men and women need to stop corrupting young boys and girls with all of their negative traits. Some people are very bad due to the fact that they have made some very bad and poor choices. These choices and decisions have destroyed most of their lives. Like the saying goes that misery loves company, now these individuals seek to destroy our children. We must go on the offensive to combat this. Now

that we know what the problem it; we must focus on aggressive but well thought out actions to save our kids.

12) There is too much emphasis on sex in black culture. The real issues ought to be re-establishing love, faith and trust in our relationships. This notion of getting your "freak" on is unacceptable. Its implementation has created a social flap within our culture in that: both males and females are confused as to what their real roles in life really are. We are re- advocating a necessary and sufficient simple rule: one man one woman. Sex was given to us for procreation and finding a soul mate that you could compliment yourself with and make a worthy contribution to society. It was never met for intimidation and manipulation of each other. The body is a temple for enjoying real love and life. It was never meant to be used as a tool of social destruction.

13) Black men and woman who have families should understand that their families come first but that we all must be ready to uplift all of our brothers and sisters who are down and really need help. It is in giving that we truly become a blessed people.

14) Blacks must understand that in our search for the equal and fair distribution of wealth in society that all of us cannot be millionaires; but we do have a right to live life in a comfortable way. Our society was never set up for all of us to be rich. But the real problem lies in the fact there is a great un equal distribution of wealth in this country.

An Open Message To Young Black Thugs And Punks

Our race has reached a pivotal period in our racial transgression whereby it is paramount that we become a more committed people towards the positive development within our black sub culture and implementation of our race. The main problem which is confronting our people today is that we are going to have to find more constructive ways of dealing with the young punks and thugs with in our race. This is an open message to them from us. They have no future and their lives are immediately being cut short because they do not want to survive. Their future is bleak and they will not survive unless they adhere to this warning and try to make our dysfunctional families fruit able and productive again.

All Blacks Should Heed This Warning: Beware Of Sraggin

1) It is now time for a new Sraggin to emerge. He can not be that same old colored boy. Contrary to popular believe"Lil Black Sambo" is alive and well; The fact is that he never left. Sambo has been in the shadows watching and controlling our every move. He has sold us out and he has financially benefited from the illegal fruits of his labor. The time for shucking and jiving is over. The new Sraggin must become a thinker; he must cut his losses and put race, anger and hate aside. The new Sraggin must learn to become a more tolerable person and make social and cultural adjustments to his life while making worthy contributions to his race by assisting his brothers and sisters who really need our help. Our young brothers must learn that "glitter and glitz " is not the proper way to make a positive contribution to society.

2) Too many sisters have tried to raise their offspring by themselves; This notion has created a parental and maternal rift in the very moral fiber of child development within our sub culture. The perpetuation of this notion has led to the creation and development of sub zoe people within our sub culture; these individuals have zero understanding and they have made zero contributions to our society due to their negative behavior and attitudes.

3) "The implementation of the monkey across the street throwing rocks" is appropriate here. Simply stated the theory advocates life for the Sraggin as being:

    a. A road with trials and tribulations that we are constantly being faced with everyday.

    b. We as black people are walking on the road called life everyday.

    c. Each time, we take a few steps in engaging life along the road; the monkey across the street with rocks hits us. The monkey laughs at the pain and frustrations the he causes us to experience.

    d. Furthermore, the theory states that each time that we as blacks increase our steps along the street of life; the monkey across the street continues to throw more rocks at us. He continues to laugh at us for the pain and increased displeasure that he causes for us. Sooner or later, as we learn more about life and the system. We the black people of America learn how to dodge the and avoid the rocks that the monkey is throwing at us. At some point, we learn to become more self sufficient in dealing with our whole life long experiences.

4) Most of our young brothers and sisters in this new dysfunctional system have been raised by matriarchal families; The women in theses families are always in charge. Too many black males have never known and or have seen their fathers let alone have a productive relationship with them. I am of the opinion that we need strong black males participating in this mix of parenting situation. Most of the young black thugs and pimps out there have never seen and or communicated with their fathers; therefore they are subjected towards leaning to and adopting to the negative and hostile attitudes of negative black males and females. Any discussions with these individuals will lead to an immediate reaction of open hostility. I have heard some of these guys state that I never knew my father but contrary to popular believe a lot of us old schoolers as we are now called had wonderful and fair but firm fathers who complimented our mothers by the two of them working together as a team to be good parents. How did these individuals become good parents?

1) They properly exposed us to good parenting skills

2) They disciplined us as needed.

3) Our parents motivated us to become better people.

4) Good Parents teach their kids the early value of work and self discipline.

5) They instilled in us the notion that family is not everything but it is the only thing in life that keeps us really focused as to what life really is all about.

6) Our parents conveyed to us the notion of what real men are. Individuals who have learned to respect all men and their sisters as well as their mothers and others who make a worthy contribution to life.

7) Our parents taught us that before you can respect others that you must learn to respect yourself. But most of all realize that respect is not just given out to you; you must learn to earn and it really appreciate it,

8) I remember my father Marshall as being a task master when it came to teaching his boys. It worked for me and my four brothers and I believe that it might work for some of our young brothers. My mother Dorothy and my father worked as a team to raise their children. Some of the values that they taught us were that each and every one of their children had a talent. They made us understand that you have to appreciate your values in order to perfect them. Life can be very beneficial to us if we learn how to harness our negatives and enhance our positives. It is the job of parents to wish the best for each and every one of their children. Parents must lead by positive example. They must let their children know that whatever happens in life to them that they will always love and support them.

BLACKS AND THE ECONOMIC SOCIALISTIC DELIEMMA OF SOCIETY

Black's position in the economic strata of the United States has been one of serious invisibility. Blacks position in the economic strata of the system has over the years contributed to the economic development of other races but we as a race have never fully prospered from the fruits of our own labor. There are several distinct and serious variables which have led to this situation developing:

1. We have failed as a race to develop economic alternatives to our survival and natural co- existence.

2. Blacks have not learned all the derivatives and mechanisms of the economic systems of the United States.

3. Blacks have always supported the economic development projects of others.

4. Since the 1930's Blacks have refused to trust the stock markets

5. Blacks because of the horrors of slavery have not invested in business and themselves even when history supports that blacks are very resourceful and creative when ever they are provided with an opportunity to excel

6. Blacks have purchased other socialistic groups products and services; even when other blacks have the same products and services available because they have an inherent distrust and dislike for each other. We will not attempt to examine some of this assumptions in an honest but fair analysis of what has gone wrong with blacks and their relationship to the economic strata

A. Why Has The Black Race Failed To Develop Economic Alternatives To Their Survival And Continued Existence?

We, as a black people, have forgotten the notion that unless we learn to love one and another in conjunction with learning how to live together; we will have no other option but to perish together. In all of history, societies who do not learn to live and work together have been doomed to failure and the black race is no exception. This constant bickering among blacks who are envious and jealous of each other must cease and desist. Simply stated, Blacks must come to the realization that they need to develop a comprehensive conceptual framework of working together as a unit to make worthy contributions to their race as a whole. What are some of the things that blacks can do to accomplish these goals:

1. They can develop new and creative businesses which will allow them an opportunity to become more economically self sufficient.

2. Blacks can develop more credit union and banks to develop alternate sources of financing which will make the race more prosperous and competitive.

3. Blacks to learn how to take a business public and learn how to use money to make money;

4. Blacks need to teach all of their family members and off spring about the opportunities about being more financially literate.

5. Blacks need to stop falling for the "get rich schemes of the system". There are only a few people who are getting to be rich in society. Most of the successfully people in life will tell you that like Edison states that " pure genius is only 99% percent hard work and 1% inspiration.. Blacks must rededicate and commit themselves to the total survival of the race and not continuing a plethora fascination of systematic schemes to make money which they will never see.

6. Blacks need to familiarize themselves with money laundering schemes in order that they might be able to avoid people who support such nonsensical unsystematic processes. It is important that blacks try to stop looking for the get rich schemes to make money in this society. It is an acknowledged fact that honesty is the best

policy. Most people who have tried to use schemes in life to get over have ended up in jail. Not only is jail not an option; it is the worse case scenario for a black who is trying to survive in life and who wants to become upwardly mobile. The key element in life for black people is that we must try at all costs to avoid jail. This author believes that jail prevents most of our people from every gaining an advantage in life. It is important for blacks to remember that once that you are locked up with a record that the future is bleak for you. In essence, just like your credit report; your jail record follows you wherever you go and at some point; some unscrupulous person will try to destroy you for no apparent reason other than the fact that you have a jail or an incarcerated record. In all probability, it is not time for both the black male and female to take total control of their lives and become the wonderful king and queens that we used to be.

B. Blacks Have Not Learned All The Derivatives And Mechanism Of The Economic System Of The United States.

The basic premise of our economic system was based upon the law of supply and demand. Goods and services in this country are based upon the notion that there if there is a demand for them than we can utilized the American work force to development an implement the proper cash flow in this country. If we have adequate demand than we can generate adequate supply for a good and service and thus all consumers can be satisfied and than we have a positive flow of the manipulation of money. But such has not always been the case for blacks due to the fact that we have always not been in the main stream of the economic strata of this country; we were the only people that a war was fought over them due to the fact that we were a necessary and sufficient fossil of the south surviving due to the fact that we were loyal supporters of the system. Contrary to popular believe popular believe most of the southern states which raised cotton would have been un - able to survive if it had not been for the loyal slaves who followed "masters every whim" to the detail. The best kept secret which has never been told is how the" master" gave some of his most precious job positions to the blacks who were really his own offspring with both a black and white heritage. It is with great pride and adulation that whites in America brag about their family lineage. But very few in the south are willing to discuss about they black southern sisters and brothers who they were raised with and lived with; with the full knowledge that they both were sired by the same fathers. It is with great distinction that most southern blacks know that between the Indians and themselves that they are the only group that were here for a special purpose the earlier development and construction of earlier America. The problem with the Indian was that he did not adapt to white America but the slave, Tobias did. This is noticeable today, because even with the onslaught of Hispanics and other groups coming to America some have had difficulty with developing and adjusting to the American Way of life. Blacks have found a way to make the appropriate adjustment for survival. This is strange considering that both the Hispanics and the yellow man have refused to make cultural adjustments because they seem to want to hold on steadfast to the old ways of life and survive. The blacks have under gone numerous name changes such as colored, darkie, sambo, Negro and African American but above us he has survive because of his resiliency. This is not a mistake it was done from the early slave days; it was set up for the survival and continued perpetuation of a nation. One cannot destroy that which is necessary and sufficient for its own existence. In order to survive with this system, blacks must venture of into different areas of survivals. The continued survival of blacks must include forming coalitions with all groups of people and furthermore blacks must be willing to form partnerships with other groups who are looking for positive development and economic self sufficiency development with this system. Money is power and power is money. Blacks must learn that he who has the money controls all of the actions with in the system. It is ironic that a lot of black families had a lot of money in the old days. In order to bring this point to the light, this author would like to tell the story of the "Dolvaliar Family" an imaginary family who epitomizes what happened the black families of the south who had a little money some of these families were also in the north and others parts of the county as it developed. Pierre Dolvaliar married Selena Dubois and they had 12 children. Unbeknown to Selena, she never knew that her husband was a black man. He fought in the South during the War Between the States and was awarded a pension from the confederate fund after the war was over. What makes the Dolvaliars story so unique is that their offspring were always doers in the way that life dealt them a hand. There ancestors were part of a land grant from Spain which could have given them considerable wealth and fortune and prosperity instead it was sold for $50.00 and a bottle of wine. The two people who were against the sale were an old grandmother Ernestine Dolvaliar and her grandson Patricio. Patricio Davaliar who later married Claudine Lastacio a New Orleans, Black Aristocrat sought a different outcome for their 12 children. There were concerned about these children receiving a real chance to survive within this discriminatory and unpleasant world so they came up with a new and specialized plan for their black children to survive. WHAT WAS THE DOVALIARS' PLAN FOR SURVIVAL?

The Dovaliars who were children during the depression did not want their children to experience all of the horrors and deception; that they had seen as children so they immediately devised a concrete but comprehensive plan of child parenting that I believe if it was implemented today; it would save a lot of our black children from going astray. This is what made the Dovaliars good parents:

1. They taught their offspring to search for the best of everything positive.

2. They instilled in their kids mind that everybody has received a special talent from "God". But it is the job of the parent along with the child to nurture it.

3. Everybody has to learn to respect the rights of others. This is the only way to go.

4. Thou must learn not to steal and to work hard for those positive things that you want. God will bless you with more than you need.

5. Learn how to be compassionate to those who are less fortunate than you.

6. Learn how to develop a strong moral fiber in the way that you deal with others in life.

7. Do not wish for those things that you do not need and do not belong to you.

8. Forget about the "Jones". It is important that we find our own niche in society in order that we all learn to make a worthy contribution to society.

9. Enhance all that is positive in life because in the end when the negatives come; you will be in a more advantageous position to deal with them.

10. But above we must remember that the road of life is both long and hard; but that the joy comes when you are able to survive the test and win the race by meeting and influencing some of the most wonderful people along the way.

11. Family is not everything; but it is the only thing. We must remember that the love that we share with one and another as family members should carry over to the way that we treat all members of society.

12. Poverty and "being rich is the same: Some people are so poor they inaccurately look for fame and fortune to solve all of their problems. Rich people are so rich that they are blind to the needs of the less fortunate in society. The real bliss comes from the knowledge that we have that "God created us in his own likeness and image; Therefore it does not matter whatever challenges that we have to deal with in life; we must remember that were brought into this world for a particular reason and that what ever we do in life ;that once it is over that we will all have to leave; hopefully for each and everyone of us we will have made the right decisions.

Special Thoughts On Angry Sisters And Too Smart Brothers

There is a special unique phenomena which is going on in the black sub community between brothers and sisters these days. Simply stated, the sisters are angry and the brothers know everything. I have tried to figure out why this is happening. At first it was hard for me to put a handle on it until I realized that it before me all the time. They notion is now being advanced that sisters are very angry and they are hostile because they have become just like their male counterparts. Brothers who are two smart has been replaced by a sister with a serious attitude. These sisters are so angry that they take out all their open hostilities out on the brothers and any man who comes into their directional path. This is a sad commentary given the fact that you do not know how to approach these sisters because you are afraid that she might want to bit your head off; it is high time brothers realize that these sisters cannot become a part of the black community main stream because they have not come to grips with the fact that angry sisters are not the African queens that brothers should have by her side. Brothers who associate with these angry and hostile sisters are setting themselves up for social and communicational dysfunctional analysis; namely the end of his existence as a man. The angry and dysfunctional sister will completely make his life unbearable for him because she wants to destroy like a tornado everything that is in her path. She blames all her problems on the black man. Someone or something has polluted her mind to the extent that she no longer feels like the positive queen that she used to be. She has become a hunter and a predator; her man goal is to destroy the black and to punish for everything unpleasant that has happened to her in life. Sister girl like she and her girlfriends like to call themselves have developed and intricate but well devised scheme to destroy the black man. She has decided that all that is important is for her to to get what she wants and what she needs. She has a positive force of reinforcements sources who support her in her endeavors namely her:

1. Mom

2. Sisters

3. An elite group of female friends

These women are all of the notion that the black man is the enemy and that he must be used, abused and destroyed at all cost. The main purpose for the Blackman according to sister girl is for him to be a "breeder" for her children. But like the black widow spider once he has served that functions she wants him with his weak self and spiritless body she wants his destroyed. I must admit that as a Blackman that these angry sisters scare me too; you never know what kind of a bag that they are going to come out of. But I have found out one thing about these type of sisters; they are the first ones that have a need to be used and abused by the dog type of black man; this creates a waste of a potential relationship.

Now, lets us not, forget brother man who is an essential part of this communication process which has developed an immediate failure to communicate between brothers and sisters. Brother man or "Tobias" like I like to call is a verbal "Mr. Peabody." Tobias is by his own definition is super smart and all knowledgeable. He know any and all things his favorite self analysis of himself is that he knows all things and that he is super smart and that he can copy any thing from anybody and duplicate what they can do. The sad reality of these notion is that he has nothing to offer any women because she has found out that he is bonk and has little to offer himself and his woman. This black man should be compared to"Homey The Clown". And we all know that homey does not play that stuff. He is there for entertainment purposes and not there for leadership purposes. It greatly appalls me when I see little homey the clowns imitating the adult male homey. This is not what the proud black man used to be. We were once a proud community of strong brothers and sisters; now we have become a community of angry sisters and "Peabody Brothers". It makes me sick to the stomach to see what brothers and sisters have become:

He-a step it and fetch brother who will do anything and everything to make himself feel like he is a real man and She-has become a daughter of Salome who would bring her own mother to shame for what she has learned to do to get what she wants and really needs in life by using all the negative tools of no class and no integrity and she has even now become a female who dose not play by the rules because she now makes them as she goes. In the case of homey the Clown, his options are not to rosy; for instance he possible faces the following if he does not get his act together:

  a. jail

  b. drugs

  c. unlimited options as a breeder with no sense of where his offspring are

  d. Being for ever tapped in the bottomless pit of life

A Word Of Warning To All The Pretty Young Things Out There!!!!!!!!!!!!!!!!!!!!!!!!!!!!

One day that fine beauty body of yours is going to be on the declined and the eyes that you once commanded are going to deteriorate and you are going to wish that you had a real decent man and soul mate. My suggest to you is that you learn how to tell a good man from a bad once and also try to learn all that you can out of life that is positive. Develop positive and fruitful relations with good people; do not be too eager to learn life to fast. Take life at pace slower than full throttle and putting the metal to the peddle. Check all these brothers out fully in order that you really learn what he is all about.

To All You Brothers Out There

Please stop beating on these sisters and start to show her more respect even if she does not respect herself; I believe some of these sisters are on the verge of suffering a minor breakdown because they cannot handle all the pressures of life because she does not have a strong man behind her. Brothers you must learn to respect Safire and appreciate her. She really needs you and vice versa with you. And both brothers and sisters need to stop lying to each other. It is high time that we start dealing with telling the truth to each other; if we don't we face the possibility of our race being destroyed.

Why We Cannot Get Along Together?

There is a strange phenomenon when it comes to understanding Black people and their relationship to one another. It is obvious to most observers that black people have an emotional problem with each other. They seem to have a precarious understanding of what it means to love and trust one another; they are quick to judge and analysis each other. The black man and woman as they exist today are in a confused state of emotional understanding. It is very hard and difficult to get any two blacks to work with themselves because they are in a constant state of flux and instability to when it comes to understanding and trusting each other. Over the years I have seen blacks move from a race of solidness to one of instability and in comprehensive of understanding about what our race is really all about. It is clearly evident that we like the rest of society have become people who do not understand what real life is all about; namely learning how to trust and love one another. I have found that the key to an energetic life is one's ability to live life to the fullest. The only disadvantage that a person has in life; is his ability and direct refusal to learn several distinct and important notions maximums of life:

1. Treat everyone as well as you would like to be treated. Some people believe that there is no value in treating people nice. I believe that the nicer that you treat people makes it more accessible for you and that individual to get to get along in a positive relationship. All blacks need to go back to this old fashioned life style.

2. Live life to the fullest and enjoy yourself because when it is over; it is over. I believe that we should try to everything possible within our short life span to live a quality but enjoyable and we must always remember that life is what you make of it.

3. Learn to make a worthy contribution to life; this notion leads us to understand that a life in which you were a contributor makes the world a better place.

4. Enjoy your dreams because dreams become a reality.

5. Behind every good Blackman; there exist a good woman and vice versa.

6. Love your children and teach them how to be positive and how to love one and other properly.

7. Remember that the world is a big place and that we all will have an opportunity to make our impact within the world.

8. The grass is never green on the other side.

9. Treat all our women like a lady. All women like good treatment and now it is high time that the black men go back and recapture love of his women treating her like a lady.

10. Beware of the black scoundrels. These are the people who just want to use and abuse you. They have no intention of treating with love and honesty.

11. Love and total commitment is the answer; Unless we have a reason to live; Our race and we as individuals are doomed to die.

12. Stop being selfish and start learning how to live.

13. Teach our young black children all of our better traits; learn how to enhance the positives and eliminate the negatives.

14. It is depressing to leave in a world whereby all blacks what to get paid for everything that they do matter how insignificant that it is.

15. Men and women should stop trying to be players and star learning how to be for real.

16. It is time to stop believing the hype.

17. Brothers should stop fooling themselves and they should start being held account for their mistakes and start becoming more responsible for their actions.

18. Women should stop hold all black men responsible for all of their problems.

19. The race as a hole has a lot to be held accountable and responsible for. It is my believe that as long as we have one black man and woman who is discriminated against in society that we have not accomplished anything in life. Are we responsible for our own brothers and sisters? I tend to believe that we are. So many times, in life when I ran into a stumbling block; I was always rescued by my faith in God and some good guardian angel who was sent to my aid. I have never forgotten that assistance and I have tried in my own special way to assist others like I was helped. Black people have to learn how to love one and another again. So many people are dying within our race to day who have done nothing to help themselves and or others. This selfish on their parts have gravitated to their offspring and have left out race with a huge void in life to fill. I tend to understand why it happened that we are now in a dark hole of miscommunication in life. People in our race have lost hope because someone has convinced them God is dead. God is not dead; He is alive and well it is we, the black people of America who are dead because we have lost our since of spirituality and wholesomeness. Religion and not just going to church on Sunday and shouting and hollering. It is living life everyday with trying to be Godlike and spiritual in everything that you do each and everyday; It does not matter whether your neighbor does not want to do what is right; you as an individual has a responsibility to do what is right. We all know why to many people have die and lost every thing so that the black man could get a chance in life to survive and to be treated as an equal. Even Jesus in his biblical teachings told us that we should enjoy the good things that God has given us; but that we should remember that when they are gone; they are gone . The key to being a well rounded man and or woman is:

a. To learn how to be patient with others.

b. To develop more comprehensive skills with our learning process for contributing positive accomplishments within society.

c. Engage with a faith and spiritual quest to learn who we really and what we are really all about; and why we are really on earth.

d. We should stop seeking our neighbors wife and her husband

e. Stop trying to copy each other and learn how to work together in order that we can make worthy contribution to society.

The Elimination of the N-Word

The N-word needs to be eliminated from the American lexicon and library all together. The word has a negative connotation and it is very offensive and it reminds black people of a very negative and depressing period in life; namely the implementation of the institution of slavery. This is very important for blacks to save their race and for them to become stronger as a race of people. But even more important than the elimination of the word from the American English lexicon; it must also be eliminated from the black vocabulary, too. Before blacks demand that it be eliminated from white society; they the blacks must be willing to eliminate it from their own verbal library of words. Blacks get offended when whites and other non blacks use it because feel that the N-word connotes racial and discriminatory verbiage and usage and for the most part it does. But whites and non whites contend that blacks state the word unequivocally to each other and it means different things such a black female referring to her man and or another back to one another as call his or her friend. But in order for all of America to be totally free from the acceptance of the negative connotations of the N-word; we must all agree that all Americans should eliminate and delete this N-word from all of American English lexicon. This is a word that we cannot have a double meaning for; simple stated it is offensive and should not be used by any one. Also, the word Sraggin should be eliminated from black and white culture. This word is the N-word back wards and it is used by many of the young blacks, black gang members and the youth hip hop counter culture. As a young black in America the warm love embrace and social and political support that we blacks used when supported each other; The word was part of a warm support that we used to support each with the movement towards the elimination of racial in equality within the American System of government and the fight to seek equality and systematic access for all persons. The word as it exists, should be taken out of every American slang, colloquial and English vocabulary period. It is very important that this word be taken out of its very existence in society. Our black race needs positive influences and the elimination of the of the N-word with contribute to this My personal advice to all persons within America is that we need to disable the N-word altogether and do not allow any one to use it; whether privately and or publicly because it has a negative connotation to it. It is also a rallying cause for hate groups to use to perpetuate racism and discrimination against other people regardless of race color and or creed. I have deleted it from my vocabulary and I hope that others within all walks of life will delete it also. One of the key elements in any one living a quality life is that we learn to be fair and upfront in all of daily dealings with one another. It is hard to be successful in life if you do not try to be fair and honest in your daily dealings with others. The perpetuation of the N-word shows a genuine lack of respect for increasing the quality of life for all Americans. It is high time that we as Americans start to deal with what is right and fair and judicious in society. As a young man, I saw so many black men who were weak and utilized the theory of the non person whereby they felt that they had all the answers to the making the black sub culture a utopian society. There is no concrete answer to what is wrong and right in society; and strive to eliminate all the negatives in society. It is high time that both black men and women realize that they should stand up and be counted for. The main goal should be for both of them to become productive members of society. Time and the system wait for no one. It is time for a new Black to emerge; the positive thinker and social contributor who wants everyone in society to enjoy the positive benefits of what America has to offer everyone who comes here.

Farewell To Uncle Tom And Lil Black Sambo

Contrary to popular belief " Lil Black Sambo and Uncle Tom" have not left the black sub community. Throughout the history of the Black sub community these two individuals have been perpetual characters in the destruction and improvement of the black race as it has sought racial equality and equal access within the American social system. It is important that we coin definitions for both of these characters: "Lil Black Sambo"- is the worst kind of black man and woman that can exist. There total goal and occupation is to put both the white race and black race against each other. Sambo uses racial discrimination and stereo types to perpetuate racial disharmony and racial strife among blacks and whites. Sambo works in harmony with other dissident groups to create problems within the races. The sambo games are organized to create distortion to enable Sambo to reap financial benefit. There is nothing that the Sambo will not do to create a financial situation for himself.

Uncle Tom-is a black person who will sell out his own mothers and fathers as well as their brothers and sisters for personal gain. Tomas as they are called with the black sub community are very cleaver and resourceful people. These blacks have been able to manipulate and maneuver with in the black and American systematic process through the use of deception and total destruction of all the positive elements of what really being black is all about.

Examples of Lil Black Sambo:

Mike-is an attorney who works for the DA office in Smooth Town. He works in a metropolitan town in the South. He handles over 100-200 cases a year. In his job as an assistant DA he over see a lot of people in cases that are questionable; but for some strange reasons he hates to search for the truth. Mikes main problem is that he hates to search for the truth because he hates his own race. He knows that he wants to gain upward mobility in his job therefore he goes along with the status quo. The sad commentary here is that Mike knows that he is bias in his searching for the truth but because he does not have any morals and scruples he does not care about searching for the truth. Mike is one of the most dangerous Sambos because he does care whom he hurts or destroys even if it means destroying members of his own race. "Al "T"- Was a six foot four inches tall black man from a large state on the west coast. His was the product of foster homes and he had a huge temper which made him constantly angry all of the time. He had a proclivity for always saying, doing and implicating the wrong things at the wrong time. But it was his anger about being black and his inability to communicate with others which made him difficult to deal with. T smoked drugs and stole other people persons possessions and on top of that Albert was a student at a college university under a disadvantaged student program. This is not to state that the program in itself was bad because a lot of students from the wrong side of the tracks entered in to the program and they did fairly well. But is the story of Al T which is necessary and appropriate for the illustration of this story and subject matter. Al T was the ultimate Sambo. Al would pimp and sell his own mother and father if he could. Al would at the mere presence of a any person from another race would advise and cajole any black person to give in to negative or inappropriate behavior because he simply hated himself and anything which advised a black to be positive within the system.

Boss Dog-Mr. Dog worked for a Midwestern bank. During the initial start of his financial developmental career; Dog started off his job employment as a bank teller. The highest position that Dog ever achieved within the banking industry was that of senior bank teller. Mr. Dog had a great potential for selling out his fellow African Americans on his job because he wanted to see all blacks destroyed and shipped back to Africa. Dog had a great propensity for disliking and hating his own people. Dog felt that in order to survive with the majority society that he Mr. Dog had to have hostile inner feelings towards himself and his fellow blacks. How did Dog accomplish this? Mr Dog accomplished the inner destruction of his own race in the following manner:

1. Dog would steadily convey to his fellow blacks that you cannot succeed within the system because you are what you and not what you are supposed to be.

2. Mr. Dog would not contribute any thing positive to the incremental and final development of the black race. This was steadily emphasized by his continued involvement with always trying to tear down all of the positive development and awareness activities of positive black people. His intense inner anger enabled him to do this.

Examples of Uncle Toms'

Throughout the history of the black race, the name of "Uncle Tom has always been around because Tomas as we in the black community have always known him always seem to be self sufficient and self surviving. The goal of Tomas has always been the same. What is it that Tomas wants to do:

1. Tomas wants to destroy any and everything which is positive within the black sub community. He will try to confuse and distort any and every thing of positive awareness and which can be beneficial to the black community and society as a whole.

2. Uncle Tom also has used a Machiavellian approach in the way that he has systematically destroyed the black sub community like a wolf in sheep's clothing Tom has pretended to be what he is not; a real man who has committed to provide positive commitments and contributions to his community.

3. One of the greatest mechanisms of Uncle Tom is that he tries to convey the notion that he is as good as other people. In essence, Tomas is not, because he is all out for himself; he has no real notion of what being a strong black man is all about. Tomas is all wrapped up in his on self surviving tendencies. I believe that in the end that Tomas will be defeated because he has nothing more to offer anyone but the totally destruction of the black race and black sub culture as a whole.

4. It is high time, that all black members of the black sub community start to say good bye to both Uncle Tom and Lil Black Sambo because both are rudiments of our past and they have no inherent relevancy to our future. It is high time that America moves on to the future. There is no time in the present or the future for these negative cohorts. This is the time for America to heal and she cannot heal with negative components within the black sub community. My instructions to both of these negative sub community components is that like in the bible; the master states that they be gone. Our positive and innovative system has no need for you. I have lived a wonderful life as a black person; it has not always been pleasant but I have enjoyed the thirst and the challenges of striving to win the good fight and meeting the positive challenges which life has to offer. The great social inventor and innovative Thomas Alvin Edison once stated that most people miss out on opportunity because it looks like hard work and; it comes to then dressed up in over alls. This is a great quote for black sub community members because too many of them give up at the last moment which when victory is upon us and actually within our grasp. In my life time, I have lost many things that I have really wanted because I have sacrificed the component parts for the greater good of the whole; I have realized that this is a sufficient and necessary component part of the survival of a race. I saw my parents, older brothers and sisters and immediate family and friends suffer great complications of life to enhance the greater internal constitutions of the young offspring to make the world a better place. It the black sub community as a whole is to survive within the very nature of the body politic and the community. All blacks, must put their self own ambitions asides and learn how to work together and love one and another; it is time to put the petty self serving goals to the back burner and work for the positive development of the black race.

Has Education Failed Both White And Black America?

I believe that in the end that the survival of Black America will depend on how we deal with the issue of education of all Americans citizens. I, pose the question has education failed White and Black America? Without hesitation, I contend that it has. The new students is of all races today; within our educational system they are all confused and they are all angry. Why are they angry? They are angry because they are mad with their parents, the system and America in general because they feel that we have not left them a legacy for their future. Little do they know how wrong they really are. America became a great country through the blood sweat, tears and sacrifices of all people regardless of their race color and creeds. I believe that what is missing from our society is that we have eliminated government and the system from our teachings in elementary, middle school and high school; it is time that we bring them back.

BIBLIOGRAPHY

Reedom, James. *The Pro Se Attorney Manual: Layman Strategies In The Law*, 1st ed. Authorhouse, 2005.

INDEX